"Tales from the Top Flight"

By Chris Darwen

© The Higher Tempo Press 2016
www.thehighertempopress.com

Follow me on Twitter: @comeontheoviedo

Follow The Higher Tempo Press on Twitter @thehighertempo

Like The Higher Tempo Press on Facebook:
www.facebook.com/thehighertempopress

www.thehighertempopress.com

This book is dedicated with an apology to Claudio Ranieri.

Thank you, as ever, to my wonderful partner Jess who continues to support me whilst I keep up the pretence of football is work.

Finally, thank you to the Costa Blanca People for indulging me with my own column. Long may it continue.

26th July 2015
Peering through the transfer window, it has been another busy week across the Premier League back in England.

On one hand I consider Brendan Rodgers a crazy madcap fool with no transfer acumen whatsoever when I recall that he blew the Suarez money on the likes of Ballotelli and Lambert. Then, on the other hand, I find myself screaming "Brendan you cunning genius" when I remember that he has talked Manchester City into giving him £49m for a player with very little end product who clearly didn't want to wear red anymore. Which is it Brendan, which is it? Splashing £32.5m on Christian Benteke of Aston Villa will either give me the answer, or not I am sure.

Louis Van Gaal must know something that David Moyes doesn't. That thing that Louis Van Gaal knows must be the password to United Chief Executive Ed Woodward's email account because the Dutchman has been firing out bids like crazy this summer and turning these bids into nailed on signings. With Schweinsteiger and Schneiderlin set to make the most difficult to pronounce midfield pairing of the season, Louis claims to have a "surprise signing' up his sleeve. Surprise to whom Louis, you have been spending money like it's going out of fashion! Oh, a surprise to Ed you say? I am wondering if Ed Woodward is actually being controlled by Louis in some kind of strange puppet-like fashion. Argentine-international-who-never-quite-made-it-just-like-Veron Angel Di Maria is reportedly off to PSG having missed his flight to the USA. But back to this "surprise signing." Some are suggesting Ramos, which would be a surprise considering Benitez is adamant he is not leaving Real. Some are suggesting it might be the mighty Zlatan, whose future is apparently now in the hands of his agent. As long as it's not in the hands of your ghost-writer, eh Zlatan? The sensible money is on Barcelona's Pedro, who is available for in and around £20m. Personally, I think it might be Argentine goalkeeper Sergio Romero who is out of contract at Sampdoria. I think the surprise element is in the fact that it is not a very interesting signing at all.

Arsene has been in very serene mood, basking in the glow of being a man who has found what he considers to be the missing piece of the jigsaw. With Petr Cech the world-class goalkeeper he has been claiming was not needed, Wojciech Szczesny is off to Roma on loan.

Jose is being Jose, picking fights with the manager's he knows he can win fights with and Everton's Roberto Martinez is very much in the sights of the title holder. Of course, it helps that Everton have a very talented centre back in John Stones, who Jose would like to make the new John Terry. Feel free to insert your own John Terry jokes here. Martinez allegedly scoffed at the initial £24m bid for young Stones, but must realise that resistance is futile when Jose is bound to come back with at least £30m.

Manchester City are acting like a team that suddenly realised that they have let all their English players leave, or have lost them somewhere in the vast training complex that they have built. It will be a tough battle, but I feel that Fabian Delph might just be marginally more unpopular than Raheem Sterling when they return to their former clubs. Wait, what's that? City have also signed an 18-year-old Englishman who has played ten games in the Championship? Crystal Palace, Everton and Aston Villa must be delighted as that will be a very cheap loan signing for them in the January transfer window.

Rumour has it that Steve McLaren has some interesting dirt on Mike Ashley. Admittedly I am starting this rumour, but what else can explain Newcastle dipping into the transfer market not once, but twice, for two very talented young European footballers? Georginio Wijnaldum and Aleksandar Mitrovic have both signed on the dotted line and, not to reuse a similar joke, is great news for a big European club's reserve team at some point in the next couple of seasons. Mind you, big Mike will no doubt make a profit on them.

Ronald Koeman is doing what Ronald Koeman does, and rebuilding a decimated side in clever fashion. Except it probably isn't Ronald at all, it is more likely to be the much vaunted Southampton backroom team, led by Les Reed. Schneiderlin and Clyne have gone, but Southampton have boosted the squad with the excellent Jordie Clasie from Feyenoord and Cedric Soares from Sporting Lisbon. All we need now is for Southampton to start the season brilliantly before fading away and it will be just like it was 2014/2015 all over again.

9th August 2015
Thank goodness my Premier League Preview didn't make the cut last week. I am guessing the editor took one look at the West Ham prediction (to be relegated, yes relegated having been foolish enough to sack Big Sam) and threw it in the bin. I

am guessing that it found its way to the desk of Slaven Bilic, who then used it as his team talk for Sunday's game at the Emirates. West Ham shocked the Arsenal faithful into more silence than normal, coming away with a 2-0 victory. I also presume that the recent trend of Arsenal fans posting pictures on social media commenting on how Cech won three trophies in his first three "matches" will now come to an end. Actually Gooners, he has won four out of four – he won West Ham's man-of-the-match. Slaven Bilic may well have been lulling us all into a false sense of security with West Ham's Europa League efforts. West Ham were excellent, none more so than 16-year-old Reece Oxford who put in a very mature display as the midfield regista, normally a position reserved for a man at least 15 years his senior.

At least we will not have to wait too long for Jose Mourinho's latest "all referees hate us" campaign following the thrilling 2-2 draw with Swansea at Stamford Bridge. Mourinho and, unsurprisingly, John Terry were livid with the decision to send off Courtois after the Belgian had cleaned out Gomis fractionally inside the area. Courtois was probably thinking that he had wished the slight leg injury he had picked up in the warm up had been worse. Ayew enjoyed a scoring debut for Swansea and Chelsea were slightly fortunate in their two goals. The first from Oscar was a whipped, low free-kick that missed everyone and sneaked in at the far post and the second, from Willian, took a huge deflection off the outstretched leg of Fernandez. Swansea more than earned their point against the Champions.

Norwich certainly had more to make no comment on about refereeing than Chelsea. Cameron Jerome had a perfectly good equalizing goal ruled out against Palace, who went on to win the game 3-1. Zaha, Delaney and Cabaye got the goals for Palace who looked full of invention, particularly from the corner routine that led to Delaney's goal.

It was a tough day for all the newly promoted sides. Bournemouth must have thought they were still in the Championship when they allowed the distinctly Championship level striker Rudy Gestede to score the winner midway through the second half. Watford led twice at Goodison Park only to see Everton nick a late leveller. They will take confidence from the performance but are unlikely to be the only team that takes at least a point from the blue side of Stanley Park this season.

Suddenly the Louis' logic makes sense. Having returned Falcao to sender and sold Van Persie to Turkey it seemed strange that he decided not to bring in another front man. All became clear at Old Trafford where United showed that they will be relying on own goals to mount a title challenge, Kyle Walker firing into his own net to give the Red Devils maximum points.

Leicester are another side I have picked for the drop, so naturally they went out and took Sunderland to the cleaners, winning 4-2. Sunderland were woeful, so much so that Cattermole was saved from himself by being substituted on the half hour mark. It is never a good sign when you hook the skipper after thirty minutes, and Advocaat must have been wishing the Mrs Advocaat had objected to his suggestion that he fancied another season on Wearside. The result did remind me what a nice man Claudio Ranieri is, and I now feel somewhat guilty for calling his appointment (somewhat sarcastically) "the work of a genius."

Newcastle and Southampton played out a very entertaining 2-2 draw at St James Park on Sunday, once again giving the Newcastle fans false hope that they might compete for some silverware this time round. Georgio Wijnaldum enjoyed a scoring debut and Newcastle would have hoped for a win. Southampton had other ideas and Shane Long headed home a fine equalizer. Newcastle in the end did well to hang on to the point, as the team from the South Coast poured forward searching for the winner.

The self-confessed tactical guru, Brendan Rodgers, has come up with his revolutionary master plan to take Liverpool to the top of the table. Sign a big, strong striker and start hitting the ball long to him at every opportunity. In the less-than-entertaining 1-0 at Stoke, James Milner could have been wondering what he had signed up to, as if he had wanted to spend ninety minutes watching a game completely pass him by then he could have done it from the comfort of the luxury seats they have for the substitutes at Manchester City. It took a moment of absolute brilliance from the diminutive Brazilian Coutinho to turn a dour performance into a "hard-earned three points at a tough place to go to." On this opening performance, Liverpool are still very much a work in progress.

16th August 2015
That Arsenal crisis lasted a long time, didn't it? Lose a game to West Ham of all people and suddenly the proposed title challengers were more likely to be competing with

Sunderland at the bottom of the table. A 2-1 win at Palace however, and suddenly everything is rosy once more at the Emirates. Wenger talked of the win, courtesy of a fine performance by Alexis Sanchez, a goal from Giroud and an own-goal by the unfortunate Damian Delaney, as a "turning point in the season." Arsene my dear man, it was only the second game.

That West Ham revival, coupled with the "Reece Oxford is the new Rio Ferdinand" campaign lasted a long time, didn't it? How can you go from beating title challengers Arsenal to losing to relegation favourites Leicester in a week? Leicester were excellent, Okazaki and Mahrez getting the goals in a 2-1 win at Upton Park. Jamie Vardy caused the West Ham backline all manner of problems with his persistent running, though Slaven Bilic will reflect on Kasper Schmeichel clothes-lining Sahko as a potential turning point, the appeals for a penalty turned down.

Jose Mourinho is desperately trying to recruit a new doctor to find the pulse of his football team. Chelsea were abject, or City majestic depending on your viewpoint, in the first big clash of the league season. Last season's runners up triumphed by three goals to nil, and if it had not been for some excellent early goalkeeping by Begovic the game could have been done and dusted by half time. As it was Aguero's goal after half an hour was only added to much later by Fernandinho and Kompany. One would imagine that Mourinho might point to the fact that Fernandinho was lucky to be on the pitch following implanting his elbow into Diego Costa's skull, a move that young Diego was far from impressed by.

Dick Advocaat admitted to being "shocked" by Sunderland's dreadful performance in their 3-1 home defeat to Norwich. Having watched Sunderland for at least ten games last season, I am surprised that such form has "shocked" the manager. Surely he noticed that they were not very good in that time, and if he hadn't I would have thought last week would have given him a clue. Norwich will have been delighted and the three points gets their season off and running.

Spurs threw away a 2-0 lead at home to "Stokealona". Following the standard cliché that Barca would "struggle to do it on a cold Tuesday night in Stoke" Mark Hughes seems pretty determined to challenge that theory – five of the Stoke squad recently plied their trade at the Nou Camp. The game ended 2-2, in case anyone was wondering.

Swansea were superb in their 2-0 win against Newcastle, who were down to ten men following the sending off of Janmaat. Ayew made it two in two for the Swans and their left winger Montero is definitely a player to keep an eye on this season.

Manchester United have quietly racked up six points from their first two games. Louis Van Gaal's side beat Aston Villa 1-0 on Friday night, the winning goal coming from Januzaj midway through the first half.

One of the more surprising results of the weekend came at St Mary's where Everton triumphed 3-0. Lukaku showed signs of the form that made Chelsea want him as their sixth choice striker, scoring twice and playing a part in the third, scored by Ross Barkley.

23rd August 2015

Ed Woodward might just be an evil genius. The whole "we didn't want Pedro anyway" thing could well be a clever cover-up as Ed is trying to sign Neymar. Yes, that Neymar! Apparently United "have recognized" that the deal may not happen this side of the September 1st deadline. Or ever. They do need some firepower though, as United huffed and puffed and stumbled to a dull 0-0 draw with Newcastle on Saturday.

Jose Mourinho might be as much of an evil genius as Ed. What a cunning plan, that chat he had with JT. "John, wait until we are 3-1 up then get yourself sent off please. If that doesn't convince Roman I need to pay £50m for John Stones, nothing will!" It worked to perfection, Chelsea holding on to win 3-2 with a very impressive debut for Pedro. Chelsea owed a lot of Courtois, saving James Morrison's penalty. WBA owed a lot of Ivanovic completely forgetting how to play right back. My advice to Everton would be to block Jose's number for the next few days.

West Ham are starting to prove I am not losing my marbles. My pre-season tip for relegation are starting to play into that prediction, losing 4-3 at home to newly promoted Bournemouth. Bournemouth deserved the win, especially considering their luck so far this season. For Slaven Bilic, he badly needs a striker. Maybe he should try and sign Charlie Austin. Just go and ask Mr Sullivan to sort that one out for you, eh Slaven?

My other pre-season tip for relegation, Leicester, are chuckling at the mere notion. They are currently unbeaten following their draw with Spurs, Mahrez scoring yet again for the Foxes. But this is Claudio Ranieri, surely this form cannot continue? Spurs need to get going soon otherwise the Poch might start to feel Daniel Levy's stare burning a hole in the back of his head.

Norwich and Stoke played out a 1-1 draw at Carrow Road. Norwich will be happy with their start to Premier League life and Stoke will not be so happy with theirs. Mark Hughes has invested a lot of wages, if not transfer fees, in this squad and they need to get a win on the board pretty sharpish.

Sunderland, incredibly, have a point on the board. Swansea will have busted many an accumulator this weekend by letting the Mackems off the hook at the Stadium of Light, Defoe equalizing for Sunderland following Gomis' strike in first half injury time.

Watford and Southampton played out the sort of nil-nil draw that makes you grateful that most major broadcasters chose to show Manchester City maintain their 100% record at Goodison Park, beating Everton 2-0. Yaya Toure looks like he has woken up from his season long slumber and the rest of the Premier League may have to beware.

Palace will have been delighted to get their second win of the season, Sako notching a very late winner at Selhurst Park against Aston Villa. Villa might feel Palace were lucky to win, especially when Pardew admitted he wanted to sign a left back and his chairman went and got him the Malian winger. Plus, Sako wasn't going to play until the passing of Bolasie's father on Friday meant he was unavailable. Fate hey, it can cost you points.

30th August 2015
In the past I have half jokingly suggested that Alan Pardew could be a future England manager. Not in this column, admittedly, as it may have led to me never getting to write it, but I have said it out loud. Today it does not sound as stupid as it sounds, hey? Pardew is now the first manager to beat Mourinho three times in the Premier League. He is also English, English I tell you. In the classic debate of "were Palace really good or were Chelsea really bad?" Palace were 2-1 victors at Stamford Bridge. Jason Puncheon, again English, dominated the Chelsea midfield in a performance that I would hope Roy Hodgson might take a look at. The Palace goals came from Sako, beating Ivanovic at will throughout, and Joel Ward. Falcao scored his first for Chelsea, who now sit in 13th.

Manchester City took full advantage of the slip, seeing off Watford comfortably 2-0. Raheem Sterling paid back a tiny instalment of his £49m transfer fee with his first goal for the Citizens. With City making such an impressive start, it makes me curious as to where Kevin De Bruyne is going to fit in. Sterling, Silva and Aguero have started the season wonderfully and there is an understandable concern that another huge signing, £51m, could upset the somewhat oil-rich applecart.

Anyway, a disruption in the City fluency would suit Leicester right down to the ground as they continue to plot their own title bid. They are about to exit August unbeaten, which was unthinkable when the season kicked off, and they snatched a late draw at Bournemouth courtesy of a Jamie Vardy penalty. Bournemouth, again, will have been disappointed not to have taken all three points but the start to their maiden voyage in the Premier League has been very encouraging.

There is not just one English manager impressing in the top flight this season, there are two! No Steve Mc, you only have two points, I am not talking about you. Step forward Gary Monk! Yes, Mr Monk completed the treble over Manchester United on Sunday by beating them 2-1. Louis Van Gaal was outraged, claiming his side had completely controlled the game. Yes Louis, but that is only relevant if you actually score more goals than them. Andre Ayew again looked like a shrewd signing, scoring once and creating one for Gomis. Wayne Rooney failed to score in his tenth successive Premier League match since 2003, a stat that does nothing other than remind you that he has been playing football for a very, very long time now.

West Ham will be hoping that the team can continue this amazing form away from Upton Park next season, when they move to the Olympic Stadium. On any other Saturday, this would have been the shock result, Bilic's unpredictable side rocking up to Anfield and rolling the opposition over. This was West Ham's first win at Anfield in fifty two years. Feel free to insert your own Beatles cliché here. West Ham have a real talent in Payet and it was he that pulled the strings that led to Liverpool's implosion. Lanzini, also impressive and Sahko scored the other two in the 3-0 win.

Mark Hughes like to experiment, I will give him that. Not content on ripping out the heart of the "Tony Pulis Way" at Stoke by signing lots of ex-Barcelona players and anyone else that is small and nimble, he wanted to show Tony that his

Stoke team could beat Tony's new Stoke team, or West Bromwich Albion as some call them, with just nine men! Stoke were reduced to the farcical number after just thirty two minutes with Allefay and Charlie Adam being dismissed. West Brom took full advantage by scoring and clinging on to the clean sheet. Tony Pulis does love a 1-0 win, even if it is against nine men.

Newcastle also experimented with playing the majority of the match without eleven players on the pitch, having Mitrovic sent off after just sixteen minutes. Arsene Wenger has often said a team with ten men is harder to beat than one with eleven, and his side were as good as his word needing a Coloccini own goal to hand them all three points.

Villa against Sunderland was always going to be an entertaining game. Did you know Sunderland scored six during the week, and Villa five? I know, and incredibly both teams conceded three. Better still, they were playing League Two opposition. Relegation candidates? I will let you decide. Sunderland went ahead, Villa came back and led 2-1 but having a lead at Villa Park is never a guarantee of three points and Sunderland duly equalised and took their share of the spoils. Scott Sinclair, remember him? Well he got both of Villa's goals.

Spurs and Everton gave me nothing to write about at all, other than to point out that Spurs are still without a win this season.

Southampton will have breathed a huge sigh of relief with their 3-0 win over Norwich. Their task was made easier with the first half dismissal of Whittaker and Pelle hurt the

Canaries with a goal in first half injury time. Tadic finished the game off with a second half brace, meaning the Saints are finally up and running.

The next few days will, no doubt, be full of last minute transfer panic buys. My tip? Demi Gray to join Bournemouth from Birmingham. Big news this is not, but the lad is a talented young Englishman who could be the next Raheem Sterling or the next Jermaine Pennant. Watch this space.

7th September 2015
There may not have been any Premier League football this weekend, but boy England travelling to San Marino gets the heart pumping, does it not? No? What about Scotland and Georgia? Come now, don't be so cynical. There must be a part of you that is happy for Gareth Bale FC's weekend results and the fact they might finally qualify for a major tournament? What's that, they've allowed even more countries to qualify so Northern Ireland might make it?

As you can probably tell, I am not massively enamored with the state of international football. Having said that, the football romantic in me really wanted Wales to follow up their 1-0 win in Cyprus with a victory over Israel. 0-0 was far from a disaster, but Wales will have to wait just a little longer to confirm their attendance at the somewhat bloated France 2016. With their remaining two games against Bosnia-Herzegovina and Andorra and just a point needed, only the most pessimistic fan could believe they will find a way of messing it up from here.

Yes, even Northern Ireland seem likely to be going with them. By the time you read this, they may already be booking the tickets. Monday night's game with Hungary at Windsor Park could be an historic night, with victory meaning qualification. To give the team some credit, their credentials suggest they might be going to France on merit, not just as one of the extra eight teams given the chance to turn up. Their seven games so far have gleaned five victories, one draw and one defeat and they top the group. Michael O'Neill has quietly and efficiently worked wonders with a squad who take the majority of their players from League One and League Two in England. There's no Gareth Bale to do everything for them in this team!

For those of you patiently hanging on to find out how England did away in San Marino, let me tell you that Scotland also had an outside chance of crossing the channel, until they lost away in Georgia. Gordon Strachan, always the optimist, still believes it is on if they can beat Germany at Hampden. Realistically, the best the Scots can now hope for is a play-off place.

Holland have imploded hilariously and will not qualify, managing to lose to Iceland and Turkey over the weekend. Iceland will qualify, having been superb all campaign.

Oh, England beat San Marino 6-0. Wayne Rooney scored a penalty to bring him level with Sir Bobby Charlton as England's leading goal scorer. This led to, naturally, all kinds of comparisons, criticisms and analysis over whose record was better, or best if you start to include Gary Lineker, Jimmy Greaves et al. "Rooney has scored more qualifying goals." This could well be down to the fact there are way more qualifying games nowadays. Sir Bobby didn't have to travel to San Marino too often. "Rooney has failed at the big tournaments." Well, only Lineker really excelled at the World Cup, and flopped spectacularly at the Euros. Sir Bobby won the World Cup, sure, but didn't exactly take the tournament by the scruff of the neck on any of his three appearances. So this could be considered a futile point. Charlton was playing in a very good England team, therefore it could be argued it was easier to score goals. Rooney is playing in a distinctly average England team, therefore it must be harder. Lineker owed all his goals to Beardsley. The point is, there are fifty or so arguments that could be considered valid. It does not matter. Rooney was clearly delighted to draw level with Sir Bobby, but you'd have to wonder whether he would rather have ended on 48, like Lineker but with a World Cup winners medal, like Charlton. "Records, they don't mean as much as medals" said Graeme Souness, once, I think. Mind you, he did win a lot of them.

Finally, England announced that their team base for France will be the £500-per-head-per-night Auberge du Jeu de Paume in Chantilly. It's famous for its links to the French aristocracy. It doesn't even have a football pitch, yet. I cannot see this one ending in tears.

13th September 2015
Leicester, eh? They are the elephant in the tree currently. Nobody knows how they got there and they are bound to fall very soon. Mahrez is, for me, the player I want to watch in the Premier League. The little Algerian sparked the revival of the weekend, Leicester coming back from 2-0 against Aston Villa to win 3-2. There were only twenty minutes to go when the

Foxes started their comeback, and it ended with debutant Nathan Dyer scoring the winner with a single minute left, and receiving a big punch to the nose by the Villa goalkeeper for his troubles. Jamie Vardy also excelled, and Tim Sherwood looked somewhat puzzled.

Some days I feel a bit like Jose Mourinho. You have so many things to sort out, you just have no idea where to start. It must be affecting the great manager, he is human after all. I mean, this is the worst start Chelsea have made to a league season since they were formed 14 years ago! A manager that looks at the current situation and decides that Jon Obi Mikel is the answer is not a manager on top form. It is one thing to be outdone by the genius of Alan Pardew, but to be outfoxed by Roberto Martinez? It's probably a good thing for Jose that Roman doesn't seemed to be that bothered this season. It is certainly better to be a lucky manager than a completely average one, and Martinez proved that when Steven Naismith had to come on after nine minutes. Three goals and three points later, the Scotsman had every right to enquire as to why he wasn't in the starting line-up in the first place.

If Jose is feeling the pressure, Brendan Rodgers must be submerged in it. A self-styled forward thinker when it comes to all that tactical stuff, Brendan pulled a rabbit out of the hat by deciding the way to beat United at Old Trafford was by having two big lads up top and hitting it long. Not that Louis Van Gaal escapes the weekend with no criticism. The Dutchman is the only man on the planet that has admitted in public that he preferred the first half of the clash with Liverpool. It was forty-five minutes of the most turgid football seen in recent years. The second half, disappointingly for Van Gaal, came to life with Blind, Herrera and then the young French signing Martial scoring. Christian Benteke had scored a stunning, yet completely pointless, goal for Liverpool and United ran out 3-1 winners.

Manchester City maintained their perfect start to the season, winning a tricky match against Palace at Selhurst Park. Having spent a fair chunk of cash during the transfer window you'd expect the winning goal to come from Sterling, maybe De Bruyne, almost certainly Aguero or possibly even a resurgent Yaya Toure. But no, in the last minute of the game up popped 18-year-old-unknown-debutant-Nigerian Kelechi Iheanacho. It was hard on Palace who had performed well, but City appear to be very determined to win back the title lost last season.

Watford finally scored at Vicarage Road, beating Swansea 1-0. Tottenham finally won, beating Sunderland 1-0 at the Stadium of Light. Arsenal quietly and efficiently saw off Stoke 2-0 at the Emirates, leaving Stoke in the relegation zone. West Brom and Southampton gave tremendous value in their 0-0 bore-fest and Norwich continued to upset those that have tipped them for relegation, which includes me, by dismantling Bournemouth 3-1. Eddie Howe, the much respected young Bournemouth manager, is rumoured to be making a move that has "sacking waiting to happen" written all over it. He is in talks with Adebayor, released by Spurs over the weekend. Don't do it Eddie, don't do it.

20th September 2015

Slaven Bilic, West Ham United, I owe you an apology. In my thankfully never published by this paper pre-season prediction piece (try saying that after you've just celebrated a win at the Etihad) I suggested, well more than suggested actually, that you would be relegated this season. My reason? Every club that has sacked Big Sam has been relegated from the Premier League the next season. You have completely scuppered my theory Mr Bilic, completely scuppered it. Wins at Arsenal, Liverpool and City do not make a relegation campaign. Forget the fact you have not won at Upton Park, you won't even be playing there next season anyway. You are staying up. You might even qualify for the Europa League. You might steal 4th place. No, I am being silly now. West Ham's magnificent win at the Etihad last night was yet another display of incisive counter attacking and game management defensively. Victor Moses fired the Hammers ahead from distance, following a neat little pass from one of the players of the season so far, Payet. 1-0 became 2-0 when Sahko pounced from close range, yet City were back in the hunt when De Bruyne scored in first half injury time. The second half could have been considered backs to the wall for West Ham, but in fact they managed to guide City to attacking into the areas that were most comfortable in defending, and with Adrian in fine form in goal the result ended up being far from a smash and grab. On Saturday night West Ham sat 2nd in the table. Yes, 2nd. That's almost as crazy as Leicester being 3rd.

Leicester City, Claudio Ranieri, I might have also said in the afore mentioned mystery article that you were also going down. Again I have to admire the way the Foxes have started the season, but they do need to get out of the habit of giving the opposition a 2-0 lead each week. Stoke looked home and dry at the Britannia but anyone that watched Leicester come back to beat Villa last weekend will have known there was more to come. A Mahrez penalty and a Vardy finish saw the Foxes grab a point and leave Stoke very much in the relegation zone.

On any other weekend Diego Costa might have made the headlines of this column. Can anyone suggest a more Jose Mourinho type player than the Chelsea centre-forward? Having successfully plunged his hands into the face of Koscielny, chest bumped anyone available in the ensuing aftermath and generally growling a lot, he managed to convince Mike Read to send off Gabriel for treading on his toes. Whether you are a fan of the dark arts or not, you almost have to marvel at the world class performance of stitching up a fellow professional, who is not the first Brazilian to have a falling out with Costa this season. Costa, named man of the match by Mourinho in classic dead pan fashion, was more effective in this dramatic passage than he was in the rest of the game but Chelsea were able to make the most of the numerical advantage to win 2-0. Arsene Wenger is still yet to beat Mourinho in a game that actually matters. The goals? Do they matter? They came from Zouma and Hazard. The game ended up being the side show.

People laughed when Manchester United paid a record fee for a teenager the other week. Who's laughing now, hey? Well probably Monaco, as United definitely overpaid because Louis said so, but hasn't Martial done well? He followed up his debut goal with a brace in the 3-2 win at Southampton. Almost as important as signing the Frenchman was sending back the paperwork late to Real Madrid. De Gea was in imperious form to keep United in the game. Southampton had led through Pelle, until Martial got two and Mata a third. Pelle did get a second for the South Coast side, but De Gea ensured that the three points were United's.

The pressure is most certainly on Brendan Rodgers at Liverpool. Rumour has it that he was told he needed seven points from three games before the defeat last weekend. Throw in a home draw with Norwich (yes, you guessed it – I tipped them for the drop) and even my basic maths tells me he is looking over his shoulder to see if those Texans are advancing.

Watford and Bournemouth are starting to find their feet. The Hornets popped up to St James Park and ran away with the three points, winning 2-1. Steve McLaren said that Newcastle are not in crisis and Mike Ashley was not heard saying "we were better than this when I didn't spend any money!" Bournemouth, helped by the goal of the weekend by Matt Ritchie, sent Sunderland on a depressing journey home seeing them off 2-0.

Saido Berahino went a long way to being forgiven by the fans, scoring the winner for WBA at Villa Park. Aston Villa are struggling this season and the Tim Sherwood nay-sayers are moving into overdrive. As you would now come to expect, I suggested they would be ok this season, just like Newcastle! Spurs beat Palace 1-0 in an unexceptional game,

I won't lie, I did not watch the 0-0 between Swansea and Everton. I would guess that both teams enjoyed long spells of possession, there were some comical moments defensively but neither 'keeper had too much to do.

Who will be the first manager to get the sack? My money is on Brendan. With David Moyes allegedly only one defeat away from the exit door at Real Sociedad will that force a Premier League chairman to take a gamble on the Scot? Or will we see Big Sam back in charge somewhere soon? Maybe one last club will roll the dice with 'Arry Redknapp? I cannot see any of them at Anfield though, but I could have seen West Ham getting relegated. Who knows readers, who knows? Probably least of all the chairmen.

27th September 2015
John F Kennedy used to say that crisis was made up of danger and opportunity. You are never that far from a crisis in the Premier League, a crisis that might lead to the bullet. Was JFK ahead of his time and talking about the lifespan of a manager in the "best league in the world?" Probably not, but the crisis-o-meter was in full swing with this weekend's match ups.

Manchester City (crisis-o-meter reading of 8.5) were totally taken apart by a brilliant Spurs performance (crisis-o-meter reading of 1.0). The game ended 4-1 and I could not work out whether it should have been more than that, or less than that, depending on how many of the goals were offside or onside. In fact, the whole confusion made the rest of Saturday somewhat difficult. The only thing that was not in doubt, Harry Kane is back in the goals so watch out.

Liverpool (CR 9.5, despite what Brendan might say) came away from Anfield 3-2 winners against Villa. The beleaguered boss will have been happy to see Daniel Sturridge back on the pitch and getting a brace, but will already be dreading the day when he is sidelined for another 6 months with an innocuous injury. Tim Sherwood (CR 7.5), however, took his whole Deliberately Play Badly Theory to a new level waiting for Liverpool to be in control before instructing his troops to start Playing Well on command. Brendan might have a point, though I doubt it. His side are only five points off top spot.

Jose Mourinho was part of the most rolled out stat of the weekend. Before the trip to St James Park the Chelsea boss (CR 9.0) hadn't won there in all five attempts. That is now six, as Chelsea clawed themselves back from 2-0 down against a Newcastle team (in a permanent state of CR 8.5) that were much improved from their mid-week cup exit. Steve McLaren wasn't sure whether to be dancing a jig of joy having not lost, or lamenting the two points snatched away. Chelsea were dire, and it remains to be seen whether Jose decides if he can be bothered with the hassle of chasing a Champions League place. Does that sound premature? Chelsea were that bad for the majority of the game.

Callum Wilson, who has been brilliant so far for Bournemouth (CR 3.5), suffered a nasty knee injury in the 2-1 defeat to Stoke (CR 4.0) which rules out any chance of the much vaunted England call up. Leicester's (CR 0) descent down the league may have just started with a 5-2 defeat at home to Arsenal (CR 7.0). Leicester had the game exactly where they wanted it, being 2-1 down at half time but Arsenal shifted into over drive. Who needs defensive midfielders anyway, hey Arsene?

Southampton (permanent CR 0) turned over Swansea (equally permanent CR 0) 3-1 and West Ham (CR 1.5) came back from behind to draw with Norwich (CR 0) 2-2. Palace (CR 0) nicked a 1-0 win at Watford (CR 2.5).

All this means Manchester United (CR 8.0 if you listen to some United fans, but really more of a 3.5) top the table, yes they do. They beat Sunderland (CR 10.0) 3-0 at Old Trafford, a game which saw Wayne Rooney also break his recent top flight drought. Sunderland fans, I am going to do you a big favour. I am tipping you for the drop.

4th October 2015
Sackings are generally like London buses. You rarely have to wait too long for one, and there is normally another one along shortly after. Brendan, if you could have held out just a few hours more then I wouldn't have had to pretty much re-write this entire column. Off I went to watch Torrevieja play thinking "that's ok, only got to write up the Merseyside derby and United Arsenal when I get back" and boom. I walk into Rodgers being sacked and Arsenal beating United in the first twenty minutes. All I pray for now is that they do not confirm a new manager before this gets published, otherwise nobody will know that Jurgen Klopp has taken the job until next week. Rumour has it he was offered it a few weeks ago. Liverpool drew with Everton 1-1 by the way, but that will be forgotten very quickly.

Arsenal? What on earth happened there? This is the team that humiliated themselves in mid-week against Olympiakos. Wenger had to field questions in the week about whether he really should be retiring. Then bang! Three clinical goals of the highest quality put United to bed and Arsenal above them into second place. Yes, second place. Not bad for a team in "crisis" after the loss in Europe.

"Lads, you are doing well. 1-1 is a good result here, just keep it tight for the next ten minutes and I reckon we will get a draw!" I cannot imagine that Steve Mc's half time team talk will have varied massively from that sentiment, so imagine his total and utter despair as Manchester City scored five goals in the first seventeen minutes of the second half to somewhat turn the game, and its outcome, on its head. Sergio Aguero helped himself to five of the six goals, his first coming three minutes before the break meaning Newcastle shipped six in twenty minutes. Next time Steve, don't say anything at all. In fairness, City were excellent and made Newcastle look far worse than they actually were, but the table is now mature enough not to be telling us fibs. Said table tells us that Newcastle are worse than Sunderland! I know, many of you thought nobody could be worse than Sunderland!

Here is my take on Sunderland's 2-2 draw with West Ham. Dick Advocaat has been making it pretty clear he is about to quit which, by all accounts, has cheered his players up no end. So much so they sped into a 2-0 lead against the Hammers, they were in that good a mood. But then they realized the error of their ways! If they beat West Ham Dick might decide to stay on after all! So Sunderland reverted back to the type we have seen all season and were dreadful in the second half, allowing West Ham to come back and draw. It only went and worked, Dick quit after the game! Big Sam and Nigel Pearson are where the sensible money's at to replace him, though I would imagine Big Sam might prefer Anfield to the Stadium of Light.

If the Sunderland players think they are being cunning, then I cannot think of a word to describe the Chelsea players. They must have really, really liked Eva Caniero. Since that incident Chelsea have been a different team, and not a very good one. It didn't look good for Chelsea when they recalled Falcao and John Terry, with Ivanovic somehow keeping his place. It looked even worse for them at the end of the game, having lost 3-1 to a good, but not excellent, Southampton display. No team has ever finished higher than fifth in the Premier League having had the start Chelsea have had.

I do love the early part of a Premier League season. Quite often you get a couple of teams that you just know will not stay at the peak of the table, but it is great fun seeing them there whilst it lasts. Palace and Leicester both won again, 2-0 and 1-2 respectively. Palace, and particularly Zaha, were excellent in their defeat of WBA and have rocketed up into fourth place. Leicester were also great value in beating Norwich at Carrow Road, Jamie Vardy getting yet another goal. Bournemouth are not getting much luck this term. Their season started in that vein with the game at Anfield and this weekend goalkeepers were the issue. Boruc made a shocking mistake that led to Watford equalizing Glenn Murray's opener and then Watford's goalkeeper, Gomes, saved Murray's penalty. With the this level of luck, combined with some season-ending injuries to key players I am starting to fear for Eddie Howe's team, not least because I suggested they might be a surprise package. Swansea and Spurs drew 2-2 leaving both teams floating in mid-table.

Stoke are slowly getting themselves together, and left Villa Park with a solid 1-0 win. Villa are firmly set in the relegation zone, and it is going to be interesting to see how Tim Sherwood talks himself out of this one. Who knows, he might even realize that less talk might be the answer.

11th October 2015
Klopp at the Kop. That is almost as perfect as Arsene at Arsenal, closely followed by the former Wolfsburg manager, Wolfgang Wolf. Yes, as I predicted in a completely non-exclusive manner last week, Liverpool have appointed the German Jurgen Klopp to lead them to fifth place in the Premier League over the next few seasons. I am a fan of Klopp, he has a charisma and charm that is hard to pull off if you are an English coach, and already he has the best beard in the league.

Sunderland managed to tear Big Sam away from his Costa Blanca villa and somehow convince him that a relegation battle in the North East was going to be much more fun for him. Allardyce was always the obvious choice and his appointment has probably increased the chances of Villa getting relegated tenfold. Why? Because they won't be able to turn to him to bail them out when they sack Tim Sherwood in the next month or so.

There were no Premier League games this weekend due to the international fixtures that saw some of the Home Nations secure their places in the largest European Championships ever. Is it a coincidence that both Northern Ireland and Wales qualify at the same time as the numbers increase? To suggest that would belittle the efforts and patronize the two small footballing nations. I mean, lest we forget that Wales are now higher than England in the FIFA World Rankings, so they must be good, right? In all fairness to both sides, they fully deserve their places in France next summer and you just know that they will only come back from the tournament with their reputations enhanced. Northern Ireland secured their qualification with a brilliant 3-0 win over a dreadful Greek side. Wales managed to stumble over the finishing line losing 2-0 with other results going their way. England on the other hand? The bigwigs at the FA must have been rubbing their hands with joy at convincing 75,000 people to part with good money to watch a dead rubber against Estonia on Friday night. England won 2-0. I now have seven and a bit months to regain some passion for the England football team in time for their imminent exit at the group stages in France.

Scotland didn't make it, even with more teams than ever qualifying. Ireland will have to battle their way through a play-off in November, having lost 2-1 to Poland in their final game.

I'll be back next week with the Klippety-Klopp of German Gegenpressing.

18th October 2015
Well then. This is the ultimate Football Manager challenge. If Sam Allardyce is to prove himself as good as his new book claims, he will have to save Sunderland from the foot of the table. West Bromwich Albion "entertaining" Sunderland was never going to be a thrilling contest, and the Baggies took all three points with a single goal from Berahino.

The weekend actually kicked off at White Hart Lane where all eyes were on the new look Liverpool, playing their first match under Jurgen Klopp. Naturally, the fans were expecting everything that was wrong to have been put right in under a week and they will have been delighted to note that Liverpool ran around more than Spurs in the 0-0 draw. That's right folks, the new era at Anfield is going to be built on running around a lot. I jest, there is a lot more to Klopp than that but it was amusing to see Paul Merson on Sky Sports trying to explain "Gegenpressing" to the average Sky Sports viewer.

Newcastle fans that might have been wishing they had not run Big Sam out of town will have probably changed their mind yet again. Their team has finally won! Quite the victory it was too, smashing the usually impressive on their travels Norwich for six. Yes, six! Wijnaldum helped himself to four in a win that will probably bring a comment along the lines of "this will kick start our season for sure" from Steve McLaren.

With David Moyes still rumoured to be looking for a job very soon, Villa Park has to look a more likely destination than St James after this weekend's round of games. Things are not looking good for Tim Sherwood once again. In the week he got the dreaded vote-of-confidence from the board, and then against Chelsea his team gave him their own personal vote by gifting Mourinho's side two hilarious goals. The first was a calamitous affair between Guzan and Lescott, before Hutton managed to divert the second goal into his own net. If the Chelsea players no longer like Mourinho the Villa players must really hate Tim.

Bournemouth were battered by Manchester City, where Raheem Sterling cashed in with a first half hat trick. This win leaves City two points clear of Arsenal, who were very effective in their 3-0 dismantling of Watford.

Manchester United did not respect the occasion at Goodison Park, where Everton were mourning the passing of club legend Howard Kendall. If memory serves me correctly, United also ruined the funeral procession the last time an Everton legend left us, the great Alan Ball. United were clinical in their 3-0 win, and Martinez's Jekyll and Hyde side put in another schizophrenic performance.

2-0 is always a tricky lead to defend with 25 minutes to go, especially if you are playing Leicester. Southampton were on the receiving end of a Foxes fight back this week, Jamie Vardy scoring his second of the day deep in injury time to salvage yet another point for Ranieri's men. They remain one of the surprise packages of the season, alongside West Ham United who got another victory away from Upton Park. This time it was Crystal Palace who fell for their slick counter attacking game. To be fair to Palace, they were looking good for a point until they went down to ten men, and then Payet took control leading the Hammers to a fine 3-1 win. That Bilic hey, turns out he might know what he is doing after all.

25th October

Votes of confidence hey, Tim? They're not all they are cracked up to be really, are they? As semi-predicted in this column last week, Aston Villa have blinked next and fired Tim Sherwood following their 2-1 defeat to Swansea at Villa Park. It was the sixth defeat in a row for Tim, who by all counts is still wearing his gillet and giving interviews about how "Tim Sherwood is still the man for this job and he will definitely turn it around." Who will take his place? Brendan Rodgers, David Moyes, Bob Bradley and (insert your own manager here, it will make little difference) have been linked to the job. Andre Ayew's late winner made him the happier of the two Ayew brothers, Jordan having equalized for Villa. They remain bottom of the table, trailing Newcastle by two points.

Is there anyone out there who didn't back Sunderland to win? They now have six derby wins in a row, and the 3-0 hammering of Newcastle was Big Sam's first win as the new gaffer. It was also Sunderland's first win of the season and puts them on six points, just two behind Bournemouth above the relegation zone. I am yet to find a Geordie that is not convinced that the referee cost them the match, Coloccini receiving a red card for nudging Steven Fletcher to the floor when the Scot was in the penalty area. The resulting penalty was scored and it mattered not that Newcastle had 60% possession, they failed to score and Sunderland got two more. Statistics and football, at the end of the day it's the final goal count that counts.

Jose Mourinho could have the only ticket in the raffle at the moment and still not win. I mean, he even lost the sack race to Tim! West Ham turned their impressive away form into the ability to beat a team in the bottom half of the table at home. A lot of the post-match noise has been about the complete lack of Chelsea discipline, Matic sent off in the first half, Mourinho sent to the stands and at least another five players cautioned. However, the real story is that West Ham deserved to win. The closest Chelsea came to looking like their old selves was when they surrounded the referee protesting Matic's red. Payet was everything Hazard or Fabregas used to be, all of West Ham's play coming through the bargain Frenchman and the Hammers had the added bonus of the winning goal being scored by the forgotten man of English football, Andy Carroll.

At some point in this season I am sure Arsenal were in alleged crisis. Then they went and beat Bayern and Everton in the same week, the latter result sending them top of the Premier League, albeit just for Saturday night. Ross Barkley had leveled Giroud's opener, but Koscielny headed home the winner before half time.

The only good thing about the Manchester derby was that Club Deportivo Torrevieja were featured in the adverts at half time! Still, even that wasn't worth sitting through 90 minutes of "Super Sunday" football. The game that should have been televised was Bournemouth playing host to Spurs. When I say playing host to, I mean kindly stepping aside and letting Harry Kane remember where the goal is. Kane helped himself to 3 of the 5 goals in the 5-1 demolition.

What does Jamie Vardy have in common with Henry, Shearer, Wright, van Nistelrooy, Stein, Sturridge and Abebayor? That's right, he scored in seven successive Premier League games (because do not forget, football did not exist before the Premier League!) Leicester beat Palace 1-0, finally getting a clean sheet and Vardy was the match winner. Palace have been excellent on the road this season, and will have left Leicester feeling like they had missed out considering they gifted Leicester the goal.

Watford surprised Stoke with a 2-0 win at the Britannia Stadium, three points that see them higher in the table than last season's champions. Mind you, West Brom are also above Chelsea, and their 1-0 win against Norwich was only marginally less painful than the Manchester derby.

That Jurgen Klopp, wasn't he supposed to bring thrilling, entertaining football to Anfield? Three games he has had now, and still unable to do any better than Brendan. The man is a fraud, a fraud I tell you. On a serious note, I am pretty sure that those darn statistics will show you that Liverpool ran around a lot more than Southampton in their 1-1 draw.

1st November 2015
TFTTF (I like that, I might use it again) has become a little like Match of the Day in the last couple of weeks. No, I do not mean the complete lack of expert analysis on the matches played or the slight smugness of the person presenting the information. I mean that we too have come into some criticism over the running order of matches. Apparently people would see some of the clubs at the bottom of the table get more of a mention, and hear less about teams pushing for the European places. With that in mind, Leicester I am afraid you will have to wait your turn. We need to talk about Chelsea!

Jose might have had nothing to say about the defeat to Liverpool, but rumour has it his players will have even less to say to him at Cobham. If I am to believe my sources, which I may as well as it makes half-decent copy, at least one player is refusing to talk to the Chelsea manager. Another has gone on unofficial record as saying "he would rather lose than win for him." Things falling apart for Jose in his third season at a club, who would have predicted that? Liverpool, however, were very, very good. Early in the game there was chatter that Klopp had got his tactics wrong by not picking Benteke from the start. Klopp was merely showing his eccentric genius, proving that currently you don't even need to play with strikers to beat the Blues.

We've not really discussed Manchester United this season, and for good reason. I am going to use my expert pseudo Match of the Day analysis technique to sum up their performance against Crystal Palace. Very, very boring. By the end of the game it was mentioned how well United had defended against Palace. Surely that should be the other way round? Palace are a solid 9th, level on points with Watford who are doing so well it can only suggest I tipped them for relegation or something. The Hornets brought West Ham's excellent away form to an abrupt end, beating them 2-0.

"Sam Allardyce will get those Sunderland boys defending much better" was the popular vote. Everton 6, Sunderland 2 might make the so-called experts reconsider that statement. The game was refreshing, as it featured a team playing with two proper strikers, in an actual partnership. Lukaku and Kone linked up brilliantly throughout, the latter walking off the match ball following a hat trick.

I only have to say Newcastle and Stoke finished goalless for you to work out what an awful day out that must have been. Joe Hart will be buying Yaya Toure as much cake as the Ivorian desires after the big midfielder bailed out his goalkeeping buddy. Hart dropped the ultimate clanger to allow Norwich to draw level at the Etihad, but Toure calmly slotted home a penalty to give City all three points. That win kept them ahead of Arsenal on goal difference at the top of the table, Arsenal beating Swansea 3-0 on the road. Arsenal's second was somewhat dubious, but Swansea never looked like getting anything from the game and are nose diving down the table at quite a pace.

Things are looking far from good for Bournemouth, as they lost again. Southampton won the first ever top flight "derby" between these two sides 2-0.

That leaves us with, as promised, Leicester City and West Bromwich Albion. The day in the life of a Fox's fan goes something like this currently. Go behind, check. Mahrez to be absolutely the best player on the pitch, check. Jamie Vardy to score in a thrilling comeback, check. WBA took the lead, Leicester stormed back to lead 3-1 before Albion made it all a little nervous at the end, getting a second. That win leaves Leicester, incredibly, in third place. Yes, third, ahead of United. I know who I would rather be watching at the moment.

8th November 2015

I did not think I would ever write a paragraph like this. In a pub in Leicester, there will have been a couple of Foxes fans genuinely discussing what results in the Villa vs. City and North London derby matches would suit their title challenge best. Why? Because on Saturday night Leicester sat top of the pile. This is not a "one match of the season played so it does not really count" thing. The Premier League is now twelve matches old, almost a third of the season has gone by in the blink of an eye. Leicester are this season's "they can't keep it up much longer" story. I would imagine those two fans in the pub would have been pretty happy with draws in the afore mentioned fixtures, meaning that the Foxes sit third just one single point off top spot.

Jamie Vardy scored for the ninth league game in a row to help Leicester beat Watford 2-1. Spurs fans would have no doubt been thinking how pleased they were to have got rid of Gomes after his goalkeeping error gifted the Foxes the lead, which was unfortunate considering he has been superb so far this term. Twenty four hours later, Spurs current custodian Lloris fumbled a relatively saveable effort by Kieron Gibbs at his near post to allow Arsenal to claim a point at the Emirates. Harry Kane took another step towards showing people he is not a one-season-wonder by opening the scoring in the 1-1 draw.

A couple of weeks ago you would have expected City to knock in a hatful against Aston Villa. New boss Remi Garde has been in charge a matter of days and managed to come up with a formula that actually kept a clean sheet, not something Villa fans have been used to. That formula? Drop Lescott, who has been woeful, and tell Guzan he is invincible. Who'd have thought it was that simple? It worked and Villa became only the second team to shut out City all season.

The other team to do it? Those goal machines up at Old Trafford. Be honest, is there anyone that was looking forward to United and West Brom? It had bore draw written all over it until a fantastic strike from young Jesse Lingard opened the scoring, United ending up 2-0 winners and sitting pretty in third place. Two goals in a game for United! Careful Louis, you'll be in danger of entertaining the fans next.

What sound does a Liverpool bubble bursting make? Insert your own Klopp related gag here. Liverpool's passionate gegenpresser suffered his first defeat as the Anfield supremo on Sunday, his side falling 2-1 to Crystal Palace who were once again far more effective on the road than at home.

Norwich got a valuable win against Swansea, and it will be interesting to see how quickly the "Garry Monk is a cracking young manager" narrative changes to "Monk needs to go, now!" It was a valuable win for Norwich, as was Newcastle's victory over totally luckless Bournemouth. The Cherries dominated but could not score and Newcastle picked up their first away win of the season. Eddie Howe could also find himself under pressure too if results do not start to pick up, though that would smack of complete short-sighted, short-term thinking that club owners would not dream of getting caught up in. Would they?

West Ham and Everton shared the points, a fine goal from the Hammers Lanzini being cancelled out by Lukaku. Sunderland losing to a Southampton penalty sounded like a dreadful game, and Big Sam may already be wishing he was back on the Costa Blanca.

This week I have saved the best for last. Chelsea. Oh, Chelsea. Never before have a title holding side lost seven of the first twelve matches the next season. It must have been bitter-sweet for Jose this week. If they win, whilst he is watching the game in the hotel, then does it say that the players do better without him? If they lose, should he be sacked anyway? They lost, of course, 1-0 to a reasonably impressive Stoke side. I know John Terry won't listen to this opinion because he is very particular about who's opinions are valid, but in my opinion Chelsea are done. They will not make the Champions League and there will be more embarrassing tantrums along the way. The season, and some respect, might be saved by a wise old head coming in as an interim. Carlo, Guus, Fabio. You know who you need to be calling, you know, just to let him know you're available. Or Sven. Oh, I'd love it to be Sven.

15th November 2015
The more eagle eyed amongst you will have realised that there was no top flight football in the major leagues this weekend, due to it being an international week. "Hurrah!" cried all the managers of the Premier League as the vast majority of their personnel flew all around the world to play in meaningless fixtures that nobody, including the players, seem to care about that much anymore. Ireland, I exempt you from the last statement as you found a cunning way of playing more matches that mean something by failing to qualify automatically for Euro 2016.

You might sense that I am not a fan of international friendlies. You would be wise to sense this. I give you exhibit 'a' as to why they are a complete waste of time, in my humble opinion. Jesse Lingard has been called up to the England squad to play France on Tuesday. Lingard, 22, (he plays for Manchester United just in case you didn't know and, frankly, nobody could blame you if you didn't) has played a total of four times in the Premier League this season. Yes, four times. Nathan Redmond plays for Norwich, and plays very, very well for them. According to most leading football websites Redmond is only second to Robbie Brady in terms of performance at Norwich and is considered, by the very same websites, to be the fourth highest performing English midfielder in the Premier League. Has he been called up? Of course not, he plays for Norwich. Another one much higher on the performance lists? Danny Drinkwater of Leicester. Called up? Not a chance. Leicester maybe higher than United in the table, but they already have their token player in the squad. Having two would be crazy! Marc Albrighton, also of Leicester is performing much better than Oxlade-Chamberlein of Arsenal. If fit, which one would Roy choose? Finally, then I shall move on I promise, Jack Cork is playing better than Michael Carrick. Which one is Roy likely to choose to play at the base of his midfield? I have veered slightly from the original point of exhibit 'a'. Caps are thrown around like confetti to the latest young thing playing for one of the top clubs, whereas players of a higher performance level playing for a less fashionable club have to wait, wait and wait some more. If Roy picked some of them, I might have been interested in the 2-0 defeat to Spain and the likely dull draw with France at Wembley.

Ireland, in the fog, got a valuable 1-1 draw away in Bosnia-Herzegovina which gives them an excellent chance of joining every other country, bar Scotland, from playing in France next summer. Robbie Brady's goal means that Ireland will progress if they keep a clean sheet in the return game on Monday night. Having said that, their defence includes John O'Shea so I would suggest O'Neill sends the lads out to get a couple on the scoreboard.

Wales showed they can score goals without Gareth Bale, but lost 3-2 to Holland in a friendly. Hello to our Scandinavian reader! Sweden beat Denmark 2-1 in a play-off to put them in the box seat to qualify through the back door. Hungary rolled back the years to the 1950's with a fantastic 3-1 aggregate win over Norway. Northern Ireland continued their party, beating Latvia 1-0 in a friendly.

So all eyes will be on Ireland on Monday night and there will be some other matches that will probably include some debuts that will end up being "one-cap wonder" quiz questions in coming years. I cannot wait for the Premier League to recommence so I can watch Jose continue to self-combust.

22nd November 2015
Wow readers, where to start? So much football, far too much for this titchy little column to do justice. Ireland! Sweden! Barcelona! Vardy! Chelsea (yes, Chelsea!)

Settle in then, we haven't got much time. Ireland will join the Euro 2016 party having seen off the somewhat feeble efforts of Bosnia last Monday. Their first came from a dubious handball, leading to an Irish penalty. Funnily enough, the Irish didn't complain this time. That's a little nod to the France incident a few years back, just in case you were wondering. They will be joined by FC Zlatan, otherwise known as Sweden. The talk before the Scandinavian derby had been about the big man retiring from international football if Denmark won the play-off decider. In the end, and to quote Zlatan, "he retired Denmark" as his brace sent the Swedes through.

I only have one thing to say about El Classico. That assist by Neymar. There may not be anything so simply beautiful for the rest of the season. Actually, I do have something else to say about it. Rafa, you have spent your whole career picking defensively minded teams. That was not the match to suddenly try and be Pep.

On to the real football, the Premier League. What a weekend, especially if you are German with a super cool beard or an ex-lower league striker now doing the business at the top of the game. Jamie Vardy, I salute you. Scoring in ten consecutive matches in one season for Leicester far outweighs scoring in ten consecutive matches over two seasons for Manchester United. You are a winner sir, your prize will be a move to a big club where you shall spend the next two seasons on the bench barely getting a look in. Leicester battered Newcastle 3-0 to leap to the top of the table, taking advantage of the City and Arsenal losing.

It is hard not to draw attention to the Raheem Sterling tweet after he left Liverpool for the Etihad. "Let's see if I made the right decision come Nov 21" it said. I'll just leave that there, no further comment is needed. That whole running around more than the other team thing is really starting to pay off for Liverpool. Turning over City 4-1 away from home, courtesy of a frenetic yet breathtaking opening half an hour, will raise the expectation on Klopp but he seems to be relishing the challenge. Firmino and Coutinho looked like the kind of flair Brazilians that would never get a game in the Maracana nowadays as they tore the champions to pieces.

Can there be a more frustrating club to follow than Arsenal? Stunning one moment, abject the next. They lost 2-1 at the Hawthorns to leave Arsene baffled. To make things even worse for the Gunners, the one decent defensive midfielder they have, Coquelin, managed to damage his knee ligaments and looks set to be out for a while. That's why everyone suggested buying another one Arsene. United looked like they had thrown it away at Watford, Troy Deeney scoring a late penalty to draw the Hornets level but then realised the error of his ways by scoring at the other end to give Van Gaal's men all three points. United now sit in second place.

Garry Monk would have been close to clearing his desk at half time as Bournemouth raced into a 2-0 lead in Wales. Swansea rallied though, and managed to get themselves a draw. Bournemouth need to start winning and soon, otherwise their stay in the top flight looks destined to be a short one. Remi Garde might also be seeing his Premier League manager status cut short. Ross Barkley and Romelu Lukaku took Aston Villa apart 4-0 to leave the Frenchman bottom of the table and looking for his first win. Stoke are quietly being efficient, Bojan scoring the winner on the south coast against Southampton.

Tottenham are doing what Tottenham do. Whereas Arsenal always threaten their fans with mounting a serious title challenge, before breaking their hearts, Spurs tease their followers with the possibility of 4th place and Champions League football. They're at it again, hammering the Hammers 4-1 at the Lane. Kane and Alli are in serious danger of being the answer to England's prayers as they dismantled a very average West Ham side. No doubt they will find a way to finish 5th or 6th by the end of it all.

Chelsea are finally starting to get some daylight between them and the drop zone. When you are threatened with a relegation battle it is important to win your home games against the teams who might be down there with you. Mission accomplished eh, Jose? It's impossible enjoy a 1-0 over Norwich too much, just impossible.

29th November 2015
Bournemouth, oh Bournemouth. I bet you do not know whether to laugh or cry. Last week they raced into a 2-0 lead, only to throw it away and draw with Swansea. This weekend they found themselves 2-0 against Everton. Some fantastic attacking play saw them get it back to 2-2 as the final whistle neared. Excellent work Eddie, you'll take that point won't you? Not a chance, Everton managed to score again deep into time added on! A five goal thriller you say? Patience my friend, patience. Bournemouth went up the other end and scored another! 3-3 was the final score, and Eddie Howe's side slipped into the relegation zone for the first time this season.

Big Sam guarantees survival, that's what they tell you. Well, Sunderland have moved out of the bottom three following their 2-0 defeat of Stoke. Stoke went down to ten men after Ryan Shawcross picked up a second yellow and Big Sam went all cavalier, playing with two strikers and everything. Remi Garde was recruited to Villa to also guarantee their survival, and he has his hands a little bit full. Jack Grealish may have been a naughty boy, but he is also one of the few talented players at Villa Park, so Garde might do well to forgive, forget and ask Jack to keep his side in the Premier League. Villa sit bottom with 5 points, the worst ever tally at this point in a season. It was Watford that walked away with the points, a result that sees them flying high in 11th place.

That is still higher than the champions, who have managed to string a few games together now without defeat. The 0-0 with alleged "title contenders" Spurs was far from entertaining, as Sunday's matches failed to live up to the entertainment of the previous day. Liverpool may yet make a decent fist of a Champions League place challenge. King Klopp saw his side beat Swansea courtesy of a Milner penalty, pushing the Reds into 6th place, just four points off 4th place. That is currently occupied by Arsenal, who are doing what Arsenal do, making a complete pig's ear of November. Two more points were dropped against a side they should be doing away with, and two more players were added to the already lengthy injury list following the 1-1 draw with Norwich. Losing Sanchez is a little like Barcelona losing Messi, except Arsenal don't have Neymar, Suarez, Iniesta, Busquets, well you get my point.

Jamie Vardy did what Jamie Vardy does, and that was score yet another goal. It was fitting that it came against the league's meanest defence, Vardy netting in his 11th consecutive game against Manchester United in the most unlikely top of the table clash in recent seasons. The game ended 1-1 and Leicester showed that they are not going away quietly, arguably having the better chances if not that much of the ball. City took advantage of the draw, moving back to the top of the league beating Southampton 3-1 at the Etihad.

West Ham and West Brom eeked out a 1-1 draw and it was left to Newcastle to provide the real comedy of the weekend.

Credit to the Newcastle fans that headed down to South London. Credit to Newcastle who, for all of eight minutes, looked like they might actually get a win. However, it would not surprise me if Pardew was just playing with his former employers, possibly suggesting to his side it would be even more fun to give the Magpies a glimmer of hope before removing it emphatically. Zaha and Bolasie ran riot and the Eagles ran away 5-1 winners. That leaves Newcastle and Steve McLaren rooted in the bottom three and the shadow of David Moyes looking down over St James Park.

6th December 2015
How many more weeks have to go by before we accept they are title challengers? In a race that nobody seems that bothered to win isn't it just nice to see someone having a go? Manchester City don't look bothered. Manchester United still look like they are boring themselves into submission, let alone the opposition. Arsenal well, they're Arsenal aren't they? They'll find a way of letting it slip. Spurs, not a hope. Liverpool, were heading in the right direction but losing to Newcastle can only signal a honeymoon period coming to a premature end and Chelsea? Well Chelsea should be more concerned about what's happening below them at the moment!

Therefore, arise Leicester, arise. The longer nobody takes you seriously, the better. In smashing Swansea 3-0 at the weekend the Foxes capitalised on City's defeat at Stoke and United's failure to beat West Ham to leap to the top of the table once again. The only surprise in the result was that Jamie Vardy failed to score against some very generous defenders and it was left to the other star of Leicester's season, Mahrez, to net a hat-trick and add a few more million to the January sales price tag. Don't do it Claudio, don't cash in on him. Swansea's finger is very much on the trigger with regard to Garry Monk's future. Having gone from being a "future England manager" he will do well to have Christmas dinner with his name still on the dressing room door.

Stoke-alona played City off the park at the Britannia Stadium and fully deserved their shock 2-0 win. City complained of the wind, as if it was exclusive to them. Stoke were excellent, and Hughes' summer signings seem to be gelling in an attractive fashion. Who would have thought the best way to find out whether Barcelona players could do it on a windy Saturday in Stoke was to sign a load of them?

United and West Ham played out ninety minutes of football that will not make anyone's 2015 highlights reel, giving Arsenal the chance to push up into second place. Wenger's men, traditionally capable of losing to a side like Sunderland, managed to edge past them 3-1, Giroud showing that he is the best striker at the club by scoring two poacher-like goals. Sadly for him, one was at the wrong end. Sadly for Big Sam, Oliver was the only person who looked like scoring for Sunderland.

Several of Bournemouth's players took to the press mid-week to defend their philosophy of passing the ball nicely to each other, rather than winning games of football in a style that the likes of Martin Keown would prefer. Quite right Martin, you should change the style of play that has become ingrained in a club and the players they have signed to play it because there is no chance they could go somewhere like Stamford Bridge and win, right? Oh. Yes, Bournemouth became the latest team to enjoy themselves at Jose's expense putting paid to the somewhat hopeful talk by some pundits that "you can't completely rule Chelsea out of the title race just yet!" Gentlemen, I think you can now.

Watford continue to be a surprise package of sorts, condemning Norwich to a 2-0 defeat. Troy Deeney netted from the penalty spot and Ighalo sealed the win. The strike pair have scored 14 of Watford's 17 league goals this season and Watford sit in 9th. I know, 9th!

WBA and Spurs played out the kind of 1-1 draw that smacks of Spurs not being real title challengers and Villa snaffled a rare point, away to Southampton.
Newcastle rounded up the weekend's action in surprise fashion by not completely failing to show up against Liverpool. In fact they did even better than just turning up, they only went and won! Wijnaldum's brace saw the Magpies run out 2-0 winners in a classic case of "why can't you play like that every week then?" That win alone should guarantee that there is a good sized turkey on the McLaren dinner table come Christmas.

13th December 2015
That noise you can hear is the "you can win the title" door being firmly shut on Manchester United, Spurs and Liverpool. Recent weeks have allowed some so-called pundits to talk up the chances of those three sides of making a dash for the title

nobody seems to want to win. Yes, the Premier League has been unpredictable this season and I have been far from the perfect prediction maker myself but I shall make this one and I shall make it loud and proud. The winner of the Premier League will not be United, Spurs or Liverpool. Or Chelsea for that matter, and you can probably rule out Aston Villa as well.

Why? Call me a fool but I don't think many teams lose at Bournemouth and go on to win the title. It is also advisable not to go ahead against a woeful Newcastle side at home, a Newcastle side that is more likely to win a game in Argentina than London, and lose. I would also not recommend scraping a 2-2 draw with WBA on your own patch.

No, to win the title you need to be able to put teams like Swansea firmly to bed with no worries whatsoever, just like City did. What do you mean they nicked it with an injury-time-deflected-lucky winner? Ok, then you need to be confident of going to Villa Park, never an easy place to get all three points, and go home unscathed. Arsenal managed that, therefore will spend at least twenty-four hours installed as my title favourites. Leicester and Chelsea face off on Monday night, after this column is sent to press, so I could go all mystic and predict the outcome. Or not. What I will say is that Mourinho would rather spend Christmas alone than give Vardy and Mahrez an inch of space to run into. Therefore I would imagine JT might get the evening off.

What about Watford, hey? In a season of surprise packages they must be heartbroken at how their exploits are being overshadowed by those Foxes. A 1-0 win up at Sunderland saw the Hornets slip gracefully into seventh place, the winner scored once more by Ighalo. Romano Lukaku seems to have Jamie Vardy's record in his sights as he scored for the seventh consecutive match in Everton's 1-1 draw with Norwich. Everton should have been out of sight by half time but allowed the relegation threatened Canaries back into the game. Palace may have just started to nudge some pressure Ronald Koeman's way by beating Southampton 1-0 at Selhurst Park, Cabaye getting an early winner. Palace continue to ride high in sixth place. West Ham and Stoke played out a 0-0 draw, West Ham still unable to find any consistency in their last season at Upton Park. Bournemouth's famous win over United moved them up to fourteenth. Chelsea, before the Leicester game, were a single point of the relegation zone.

Finally, who will be the new Swansea manager? Well, it won't be Brendan Rodgers who sees a move back to Wales as a backward step in his career. It won't be David Moyes, who was never in the running. Ryan Giggs is being seriously considered, though he might be better picking up the pieces at United in the short-term when Van Gaal strops off in January when he isn't allowed to go and buy a striker having sold all the ones he had. Dennis Bergkamp and Gus Poyet are also in the running, and my money is on Gus.

20th December 2015
Well folks, just a quiet little column from me this week. Not a lot has happened in the world of football. Nothing at all, everyone is winding down for Christmas. Oh that? Is that really news? Honestly, people care about that? Really? Ok, if you insist – the big news of the last week of Premier League shenanigans was King Klopp apologising to Tony Pulis for his little outburst following their 2-2 draw last weekend.

In other, far more insignificant news, that Portuguese individual has left Chelsea by mutual consent for the second time. Yes, I know this is the real story of the week but surely it has been written about enough by now? In what would have been a hilarious twist, the early rumour doing the rounds was that Juande Ramos was being lined up to be the interim replacement. Clearly Roman was having a little bit of Christmas fun as within 48 hours Guus Hiddink was announced as the man to be very, very nice to those players who need love, not shouting at. Chelsea, in the ultimate two-fingers to their former manager, beat Sunderland 3-1 in a manner that suggested they can still play a bit of football. The Chelsea fans, however, might take a little longer to forgive them.

So Jose out and then bang, the news breaks from Munich that Pep is packing his bags and heading somewhere new in the summer. Former Chelsea manager, hardly an exclusive club, Carlo Ancelotti is the man to replace him which immediately removes him from contention in the Chelsea/United/City scenario that is set to rumble for the rest of the season. I know United have a manager, but if they go around losing to teams like Norwich then they won't have for much longer. Jose, never shy, has already made contact with Old Trafford through his agents, you know, just in case. So if Jose goes to Old Trafford, that means Pep won't be going there. Ah, City you say? Well, even Pellegrini seems to think Pep is the right man to take over from him, according to interviews over the weekend. So Pep will be at City next season. Maybe. But what about Chelsea? I have no idea, other than it might well be Simeone meaning there is every chance that Pep, Diego and

Jose can recreate their La Liga rivalry in slightly chillier climes.

Still with me? Good. So what actually happened on the pitch this weekend? Chelsea won, United lost as we have already learned. King Klopp, he was supposed to be some kind of saviour wasn't he? The new Shankly? The man to bring glory where Brendan Rodgers failed? Watford 3, Liverpool 0. I'll just leave that there for you to consider. Yes, Watford are now a single point outside the Champions League places in this crazy season. Ighalo notched another brace.

That Leicester bubble just refuses to burst, and they will eat their Christmas turkey safe in the knowledge that they top the table. Goodison Park was the kind of place where wheels can come off runaway trains, but the Foxes ran out convincing 3-2 winners, Mahrez adding another few million to his price tag with another couple of goals.

Bournemouth's revival continues, departing the Hawthorns with all three points in their Christmas stocking beating WBA 2-1. Southampton are in a worrying freefall, the kind of form that could see them dragged into a relegation battle in 2016. Spurs comfortably saw them off 2-0, a result that sees the Lilywhites leapfrog themselves into fourth place. Palace are on the same number of points as United and Spurs and sit sixth on goal difference following their 2-1 win at in-form Stoke. Newcastle and Villa played out a 1-1 draw where the rain was the most interesting thing until Jordan Ayew's stunning equaliser for Villa. Newcastle end the year just off the relegation places and Villa remain certainly doomed.

3rd January 2016

We might have taken our winter break at the CBP, but over in Blighty they were forced to keep going, playing hundreds of matches in just a few days to keep that wonderful thing called "tradition" alive and well. It matters not that every other country with half a mind gives their players a winter break, allowing them to be fully charged for such unimportant things like the Champions League or minor events like European Championships or World Cups. No, the Premier League knows best and there were some clear winners and losers over the last few weeks.

Arsenal

Getting absolutely smashed in Southampton over Christmas is quite a tradition for several people I can imagine, but it was not really part of Arsene's plans. Is it possible to lose 4-0 to the Saints and win the league? Clutching at straws a little, but I recall Manchester United having some hammerings at the old Dell and still going on to lift the title. Arsenal recovered well to win the next two and sit top of the pile.

Leicester City

Liverpool away, Manchester City at home, Bournemouth away. It shows how far Leicester have come that they will be distraught that they only accumulated two points over Christmas. The team that had scored in every Premier League match up until Anfield managed to not score a goal in the three matches, and Mahrez's missed penalty against Bournemouth may well have been accompanied with the clunking sound of wheels falling off a title bid.

Tottenham Hotspur
Spurs are in severe danger of looking like they could win the title that nobody wants to win. The annual attempt, and failure, to finish fourth has to be the worst case scenario for Poch's men now having come through the last three games with the seven points. The last minute winner at Watford could be a season defining moment, and providing Harry Kane was given a lot of cotton wool at Christmas and is not adverse to being wrapped in it there is more than an outside chance that Spurs could still be in the mix come the end of the season.

Manchester United
There is little point turning up to Old Trafford before half time nowadays. In the last nine home matches the former champions have failed to score in the first forty-five minutes, and the opposition have only registered once in that time. Christmas started with a lot of talk about LvG resigning, or being sacked, and Jose stepping in and going on to win the title yet again. That talk got a lot louder as the Christmas wine flowed over the dining room table, and the 2-0 defeat at Stoke left Louis looking like he had got the worst toy from a cracker in history. They improved against Chelsea, and then Rooney won the game against Swansea. That Rooney goal summed up everything that is wrong about New Year resolutions for me. "2016 is going to be great, I'm going to start scoring goals." Why wait until January 1st Wayne?

West Ham
I could not have got West Ham more wrong this season having tipped them, and Leicester, for the drop. Regular readers will also note that I have commented on their poor home form in

their final season at Upton Park. Poor home form? Bilic's Boys have not lost at home in months! They sit fifth in the table, courtesy of a draw at Villa and then beating Southampton and Liverpool on home turf. With Payet back and looking sharp, what could they achieve in the second half of the season?

Crystal Palace

Pardew to Real Madrid, that was a Christmas cracker joke, right? Don't get me wrong, Pards is doing a very good job at Selhurst Park but anyone that thinks Frazier Campbell is a Premier League striker should not be allowed to manage in Europe. Palace had an average time of it, ending on the low of a hammering against Chelsea which was always going to happen when Pardew started talking about how he beat them last time.

Liverpool

King Klopp spent most of Christmas wondering why he was being asked to work every day and getting angry with the people he was spending time with. I have to say, if I was forced to speak to James Milner every day I would need to vent once in a while. It started well with a 1-0 win over Leicester, but trips to Sunderland and then West Ham with far less recovery time than other teams saw that be the only high point.

Watford

The Hornets deserved far more than they got. Brilliant against Chelsea, Spurs and City they ended up with a single point. They sit ninth and they're excellent season should continue.

Stoke
Much has been made of Stoke's "new found brilliance." Further inspection shows that they beat City 2-0 at home a little while ago (lots of teams beat City at home) and beat United 2-0 on Boxing Day (lots of teams beat United). Other than that, they clearly got Everton in Secret Santa and the gift was as many goals as they needed to win and they lost to WBA which nobody should do.

Everton
Everton were Everton. Entertaining and frustrating. If John Stones is worth £50m then I reckon you could still get a few million for Kevin Ratcliffe.

West Brom
Tony Pulis, I respect you as a manager and your achievements. I understand that you set a team up to play a certain way and it works for you. It does not mean I have to write about it. Six points from three games.

Southampton
The Saints looked like they were out of their slumber when they beat Arsenal. It was a bit like the dog waking up in the middle of the night, they soon go back to sleep for hours. Norwich, Bournemouth and Chelsea must all overtake them which means it could be a nervous end to the season for Koeman.

Norwich
The other team I tipped for the drop. They lost the game they expected to, and won the two they needed to. Not a chance

they are going down now, and I am going to spend the next few weeks inserting as many Ed Balls puns into this column as I can.

Bournemouth
Eddie Howe's men seemed to be like elves, only working at Christmas as their form picked up massively in December. However, two nil-nil draws and a defeat to Arsenal suggested that like elves, they clock off as soon as the turkey is finished. It will be interesting to see how they react to another mini-slump.

Chelsea
Christmas. Guus. Guus has put on some weight. You can do the rest. They won't get relegated, but they certainly won't qualify for Europe next season. It might make it tough to recruit the big name boss that Roman will want. They put in their best performance of the season in beating Palace 3-0.

Swansea
I know Swansea like to spend money wisely, so I applaud them for saving themselves a head on the Christmas party by sacking Monk in advance and not replacing him until the New Year. Whoever gets the gig will find a team defending with a little more steel but lacking in attacking confidence.
Swansea's best hope is that Newcastle continue to be terrible.

Newcastle United
A last minute loss at Everton. The debut goalkeeper throws one in against West Brom. Losing the sort of game where Arsenal are normally there for the taking. Steve McLaren must have been very bad last year as he certainly did not get

what he wished for for Christmas. Newcastle are properly in the relegation mix now, and their biggest challenge might be finding a third team that are worse than them this season to finish beneath them.

Sunderland
The 3-1 win over Villa will give the Mackems false hope. Unless they ace the transfer window they are going down. Even Big Sam is starting to look like a man who wishes he had spent Christmas on the Costa Blanca.

Aston Villa
Doomed.

Predictions are always fun aren't they, especially when I traditionally get them so incredibly wrong. Anyway. Arsenal to finally win the league. Leicester to get Champions League football with Spurs and City. Leicester to win the FA Cup. Barcelona to win the Champions League and Gary Neville never to manage a top flight club again. Happy New Year!

10th January 2016
There isn't a great deal of romance left in the world, lest the world of football. However, there is one weekend in the year where "romance" is the buzzword, providing it is quickly followed by "of the cup." This weekend was the FA Cup Third Round weekend, where the Premier League millionaires and playboys have their reputations thrust on the line and are forced to play on pitches the resemble actual football pitches, and not pristine carpets.

An eye was cast down the list of fixtures in advance to see where the potential shocks might occur. Oxford against a struggling Swansea stood out, Chelsea against Scunthorpe had banana skin written all over it and the possibility of the biggest shock of the round was at Adams Park where there was an outside chance Villa might just about beat Wycombe.

The action kicked off on Friday night, where the FA and BT Sport practical jokes department thought it would be nice to send Liverpool down to Exeter. No need for the Liverpool fans to panic, the last train home left just before kickoff. For the majority of the game it looked like Liverpool had missed the train themselves as Exeter deservedly led 2-1. King Klopp had rested the majority of his first team, those that were not currently injured anyway, and the clearest indicator of the weakened side was goalkeeper Bogdan, once again flapping at a corner and costing the side a victory. Liverpool battled back to steal a draw, meaning Exeter get a handsome little payday at Anfield and we get to see their manager's hat once more.

Saturday dealt up some surprises of its own. Non-league Eastleigh were moments away from making Bolton's miserable existence even gloomier, before the Lancashire side snatched a draw. Wycombe busted many people's betting slips by failing to beat Aston Villa, the game also ending level. There were five all-Premier League ties, with Manchester City, Watford, Arsenal, and Palace knocking out Norwich, Newcastle, Sunderland, and Southampton, Spurs and Leicester getting the result neither team wanted in their 2-2 draw. Each of the beaten sides can genuinely use the excuse of wanting to focus on the league. BT Sport, once again in their infinite wisdom, thought it would be good to finish off the Saturday coverage with a blockbuster, the kind of game that would get people off their seat. Well they managed that, a couple of million people were off their seat long before half time to stick the kettle on as United managed their tenth game in a row without scoring before half time. Sheffield United nearly held on for a draw, an injury time penalty from Rooney seeing Old Trafford awaken from its slumber and secure a 1-0 win.

Sunday started with another Premier League side falling. Oxford came from behind to knock out struggling, managerless Swansea in the biggest scalp of the round. Chelsea ended up easing past Scunthorpe before Spurs and Leicester Reserves played out an entertaining tie.

With there being a mid-week round of Premier League fixtures you will be in for a double serving of Tales from the Top Flight next week. Isn't that something to look forward to, eh?

14th January 2016

Don't listen to them Louis, don't fall into their trap. Don't let the millions of punters that bet on Newcastle – United being 0-0 get into your head. Newcastle, who had lost the last 27 games 1-0 faced United, who hadn't scored more than one goal since Alex Ferguson retired, if you believed the pre-match chat. The result? The most entertaining 3-3 of the season. What odds would you have got on that? You could almost feel LvG crying inside at such attacking frivolity.

The most entertaining 3-3 of the season tag lasted a mere 24 hours as Arsenal and Liverpool threw caution to the wind the following evening. Where United's thriller was borne more from peer pressure, this one was down to Liverpool's defensive incompetence and Arsenal's total inconsistency. Firmino scored a stunning goal which meant another calamitous goal conceded from a corner even more amusing to the neutral.

Leicester went to Tottenham, that dark horse for the title, and came away with all three points. That Leicester, if they actually want to win the title it is there for the taking. Villa did something we all thought might not happen again this season, they won! Yes, the joke was very much on Palace as they managed to go to Villa Park and fail to score. Incredible. Bournemouth looked superb momentarily against West Ham, before West Ham decided to put in twenty-three minute shift and win the game 3-1. Now, anyone who has watched them this year know that WBA are not very good. Not very good at all in fact. They are even worse to watch. Yet a trip to Chelsea is always a chance to nick a point, and nick a point they did with the game finishing 2-2.

City don't seem to want to win the title either, drawing 0-0 with Everton. Sunderland cast Swansea a hammer blow, albeit massively helped by one of the worst refereeing performances of the season. Defoe helped himself to a hat-trick in a 4-2 win. Norwich were poor in their trip to Stoke, which as we all know is not a good place to go on a cold, windy Wednesday night. The Potters won 3-1. Southampton looked like they realised they might be slipping into a relegation battle whilst turning over Watford 2-0.

The weekend was set up as beautifully as a Joel Campbell reverse pass.

17th January 2016

Leicester. Leicester. Leicester. I literally want to bang their heads against the wall. All they had to do was score a penalty against Villa and they would be opening up daylight at the top of the table. Mind you, if they had scored a penalty against Bournemouth they would already have some daylight. Claudio, some advice. Don't let Mahrez take penalties. Again. Ever. A 1-1 draw saw Leicester go top overnight.

This new Wayne Rooney is going to start giving everyone false Euro 2016 hope at this rate. An in form Rooney netted the winner against Liverpool, and United were thankful to De Gea for keeping the home team at bay. Remember when people thought King Klopp might get Liverpool into the Champions League places this season? Hilarious! What could be more hilarious? People suggesting that if Rooney keeps playing like this England might win this summer. I don't mean just a match, the whole thing. United sit in fifth, Liverpool ninth.

Bournemouth learned from the mid-week West Ham defeat and remembered to finish the job off this time, stuffing Norwich 3-0. Playing like that, it is hard to believe Bournemouth will have any difficulty in avoiding relegation, but the Cherries are 15th and only five points above Swansea who have slipped into the relegation places themselves. Still, Chelsea are only one point and one place above Bournemouth, so by rights they must be considered to be "relegation threatened," no? The best 3-3 draw of the season moniker changed hands once again. Everton threw away a 2-0 lead in the space of three minutes, then went 3-2 up again only to concede late into injury time. Those Toffee's, they like to give their fans their money's worth.

Southampton have quickly moved away from the wise man's tip of being the team most likely to get dragged into the relegation chat by winning their last two matches. WBA were put to the sword at St Mary's, a Ward-Prowse double helping the Saints to a 3-0 win.

City remembered where the goal was, putting four past a hapless Crystal Palace at the Etihad. The win keeps Guardiola's, I mean Pellegrini's, men one point behind Leicester and Arsenal. Arsenal seem as keen as Leicester to stamp their authority on the title race, drawing 0-0 with Stoke where both 'keepers excelled.

Newcastle have gone goal crazy, and the signing of Jonjo Shelvey might go down as one of the January deals of the century. That is you feel inclined to judge it off one game, or maybe the first fifteen minutes of said game. Shelvey inspired the Magpies to a 2-1 win over West Ham, playing a part in both of the opening goals. The result sees Newcastle move above Swansea, who play Watford on Monday night.

Spurs recovered well from their mid-week defeat, and were helped by one of the worst Premier League debuts in living memory. I recall Massimo Taibi letting a Le Tissier shot through his legs on his United debut. I recall Chris Sutton missing an open goal on his Chelsea debut. Further afield, Jonathan Woodgate did not fill himself with glory on his Real

Madrid debut. But step forward Jan Kirchoff. The score was 1-1 when Big Sam sent the German on to shore things up at the back. Thirty seconds later it was 2-1 and even the harshest critic would struggle to blame him for that goal. The defending that led to Jan deflecting Eriksen's shot into the top corner ten minutes later was a little harder to explain, and the tackle that floored Rose in the area was just clumsy. In just 31 minutes Sunderland capitulated to a 4-1 loss, and Kirchoff entered Premier League folklore.

24th January 2016
As regular readers of this column will know, I claim not to be much of a gambling man. But imagine if I had put €100 on under 0.5 HT goals at Old Trafford, every match this season? I wouldn't need to be writing this now, that is for sure! Yes, for the four hundred and sixth time since Fergie retired, United went in at 0-0 at home on Saturday. The opposition were Southampton, who summoned their £4m signing Charlie Austin from the bench. Austin, a former bricklayer who came through the non-league scene at Poole, had the dream debut scoring the winner just three minutes from time. United still in the title race? I think not.

King Klopp maintains he is all about heavy metal, thrills and spills, crazy mad football. To be fair to the enigmatic German, he is providing a little more entertainment than LvG. The game at Carrow Road had everything from comical defending to goal of the month contenders and when Norwich made it 4-4 in injury time you could have been forgiven for thinking the chaos was finally over. This is the Premier League folks, the only predictable element of this season is the unpredictability of it all! Lallana broke the Canary hearts by notching the ninth goal of the game even deeper into injury time. Do you remember Klopp calling out Liverpool fans for leaving matches early? That is why. Whether he can return Liverpool to their glory years I do not know, but Liverpool are going to be very interesting to watch over the next season or so.

It shows how impressive Leicester are when beating a Stoke side with their own European aspirations is not even a minor shock. With Stoke happy to have the ball and Leicester more than happy for them to have it, it was the perfect scenario for the Foxes. Sure enough, they romped to a 3-0 win and Jamie Vardy was back in the goals. Leicester have Liverpool, Manchester City and Arsenal in the next three games. If they can come out of those matches with five points or more there is a huge chance that something incredible might be happening, especially if Arsenal keep losing games here and there.

The stage was set on Sunday for Arsenal to move ahead of Leicester on goal difference. All they had to do was beat that relegation threatened team in blue. Even without Jose in charge, Chelsea remain Arsenal's nemesis, their kryptonite. After 18 minutes Diego Costa and Per Mertesacker got caught in one of those embarrassing dad races at the local sports day and the German got a straight red for bringing Costa down. Personally, I think anyone who gets out-sprinted by the slightly rotund striker deserves an instant dismissal. Costa proved to be the double thorn in the side, meeting Ivanovic's cross with a fine finish for the game's only goal. Leicester have three points clear daylight at the top.

This has to be the least Spurs-like side in history. I mean, they are consistent and winning games that previous Spurs teams would have drawn or lost. 1-1 with seven minutes to go at Palace and Dele Alli scored the kind of goal Matt Le Tissier would have been proud of. Receiving the ball with his back to goal, Alli lobbed the ball over his marker, spun, and volleyed home from 20 yards. If Roy Hodgson does not build the England team around him this summer it will be a wasted opportunity.

A lot has been said about plucky little Bournemouth and their style of football. I admit to being a huge Eddie Howe fan, but enough of the little now. Bournemouth face a huge fine if they are relegated to the Championship for failing to meet financial fair play guidelines in their promotion season. Sadly, this is tantamount to cheating by the rules laid out. Bournemouth have been able to buy big this month, Big Ben Afobe coming in from Wolves for just under £10m. With two goals already, he will ensure the Cherries stay up this season. His goal on Saturday ensured a 1-1 draw with Sunderland.

The Watford slump and Newcastle revival both came to an abrupt end in the same ninety minutes. Ighalo scored again as Watford got a much needed 2-1 win. It would seem that Newcastle are extending their inability to win in London to just north of the capital these days. Swansea capitalised on Newcastle, Norwich, Bournemouth and Sunderland's failure to win by beating Everton 2-1. The win lifts the Swans to 15th in the table.

One day someone will write a book on the greatest 0-0 draws ever. WBA 0 – 0 Aston Villa will not be in it.

31st January 2016

If you believe the television puppeteers, the FA Cup means excitement, drama and romance. The FA Cup can often be a welcome respite to those managers under the cosh. Yes Mr Van Gaal, we mean you. Premier League wise it is only the legendary Dutchman that is looking over his shoulder currently. Mind you, Louis is not adverse to openly flirting with the grim reaper. By all accounts he has offered to resign from United three times, and someone has kept talking him out of it. That someone is Ed Woodward, the man that authorised the signing of Felliani and sales of Hernandez and Di Maria. Good work Ed, Old Trafford thanks you. Anyway, United's trip to big-spending Derby County was very much on the list of potential upsets. The biggest upset was that United managed to score three times in a game, winning 3-1.

Looking down the list of Saturday fixtures, the shocks could have come from Colchester, Portsmouth, Oxford, Villa and Burnley but none were able to write the appropriate newspaper headlines. Spurs outclassed Colchester in winning 4-1, Bournemouth recovered from being a goal down to beat local rivals Portsmouth 2-1 and Oxford were unable to repeat their third round heroics, getting turned over 3-0 by Blackburn. Villa were never likely to get a result against Manchester City, losing 4-0 and Burnley will have been distraught to have lost 2-1 to Arsenal.

By this point, the FA Cup was severely lacking in excitement, drama or even romance.

Also through to the next round went Leeds who, whisper it quietly, looked like the more sensibly run club of the two when they faced Bolton. Bolton, who never recovered from losing Big Sam Allardyce, are currently marooned at the bottom of the Championship and over £180m in debt. Leeds fans may have divided opinions about their current owner, but somewhere there has to be an element of gratitude that they are not back in the position themselves. Bury never looked like beating Hull, who enjoyed a comfortable 3-1 win over their lower league opponents and Palace finally scored a goal themselves! It has not been much of a cup week for Mark Hughes and Stoke, cruelly knocked out of the League Cup on penalties by Liverpool midweek. Any hopes of bouncing back with a win were taken away by Zaha's early goal, meaning Stoke's dreams of being anything other than a safe mid-table side have ended for another year.

Last year's beaten semi-finalists Reading efficiently dispatched League One high flyers Walsall 4-0 and Shrewsbury caused something of a shock by beating Sheffield Wednesday 3-2. You know it was a quiet day when perennial underachievers losing by a goal is classed as a shock. West Bromwich Albion managed to throw away the lead twice, drawing 2-2 with Peterborough. West Brom, an outside tip to slip into a relegation battle? Probably not now I have committed that to paper.

Saturday night's televised game saw a repeat of the 2005 final, one of the better finals in recent memory. Liverpool beat West Ham that day, and everyone was hopeful of another thriller. Naturally that led to a dull 0-0, which neither side was particularly keen on. Liverpool have a fixture pile up that King Klopp continues to smile ironically about.

Sunday would give us some excitement, drama or romance wouldn't it? Everton, beautifully inconsistent, were playing Carlisle. You can imagine the final words in the Carlisle dressing room. "Keep it tight lads, it's 0-0 after half an hour they'll start to panic!" Therefore conceding after two minutes was not ideal, Everton strolling to a 3-0 win overall. Many felt that the MK Dons might cause Chelsea some problems. Sadly not, even Oscar and Hazard found themselves on the score sheet with the Brazilian getting three.

The FA Cup, distinctly lacking in excitement, drama and romance. At least the Premier League is back next week, hey?

3rd February 2016

I am starting to think the Premier League and the FA do not get on. Yet again, following a weekend round of the FA Cup, the Premier League were in midweek action possibly explaining some of the interesting team selections in the "greatest cup in the world" just days before.

That Jamie Vardy, he only scores tap-ins, right? NO! That Leicester, they just whack it long to the quick lad don't they? NO! Well, maybe. The pass from Mahrez to Vardy for the former non-league striker's first goal against Liverpool was sublime. That said, Vardy still had a tiny bit to do when the ball arrived exactly where he wanted it. The eventual volley from distance was exquisite and sailed into the net, setting the scene for Leicester to go and seal their place at the top of the table once again. With Aguero sealing a 1-0 win for City at

Sunderland, the gap remains three points and Leicester have picked up three of the five to seven points needed from the tricky run of fixtures before them.

Arsenal, having been thumped by Southampton on Boxing Day, would have been hoping for a little dish of revenge served on a cold Tuesday night platter at the Emirates. Instead the higher drama was Arsene managing to upset yet another fellow manager, this time Ronald Koeman who was reported to have said "it's always the same with you!" By this I would assume that Koeman meant that Arsenal always look like they might actually want to win the Premier League before changing their minds and offering it to all the teams around them on a plate. The 0-0 meant that Spurs sneaked ahead of their local rivals into third place, another emphatic and efficient 3-0 win against Norwich sending Pochettino's men closer to the leading pack.

Manchester United were involved in another shock result, beating Stoke 3-0. The biggest shock of it all was the fact that United scored twice in the first half. Old Trafford has not scenes like these since the "great old days" of 2012. United still trail the Champions League places by five points, and will be patiently waiting for Spurs or Arsenal to vacate.

Big Ben Afobe is already making space on his mantelpiece for the "best January signing" award. The striker signed from Wolves scored yet again, this time the winner against Palace. Bournemouth are flying, seven points clear of the relegation zone. West Ham might still cause the European places a few problems, another win seeing them comfortable in 6th spot. Villa were the victims, not helped by an idiotic red card.

Manager Remi Garde has already intimated he is considering his position as he was left amazed by Villa's inability to persuade anyone to join an already sunk ship in the transfer window.

West Brom were moments away from having the "they're in a big relegation battle now" label firmly attached to the peak of Tony Pulis' baseball cap before Rondon equalised against a much improved Swansea.

7th February 2016
The weekend round of Premier League games threw up more questions than answers.

Leicester, I have a plea from the majority of the neutrals in the football world. You had better not be teasing us, please go on and win this damn title. Leading 3-0 at the Etihad must be a beautiful thing, and they went on to win the game 3-1 meaning that they now have a gap of (insert) points at the top of the Premier League, the very same Premier League that they were rock bottom of not thirteen months ago. Has anyone mentioned that fact recently? That is six points from six points in the "tricky run of fixtures that will tell us whether they are serious contenders." I think it is safe to say they are. That Mahrez, are there anymore words to describe him?

City's defeat allowed Spurs fans to get very excitable as their 1-0 win over Watford saw them groove into second place overnight. Trippier, massively underused this season, got the winner. With all the Leicester chat, nobody has really noticed how well Spurs have been doing. Can they keep it up to capitalise on any slips?

Liverpool fans walked out in their droves in the 77th minute of their match against Sunderland. It was a protest against the proposed hike in ticket prices for next season. Klopp, early in his Anfield reign, criticised Liverpool fans for leaving before the end of the game, as there could well be more action about to happen. It certainly was the case on Saturday, the departing fans missing Sunderland's surprising come back to draw 2-2 and steal a point.

Villa are quietly sorting themselves out. Their 2-0 win over a dreadful Norwich saw the Canaries slip into the relegation places but Villa close the gap between them and survival to a mere eight points. It is still a massive ask, but who knows? The mere fact that I said they were relegation certainties should give them hope that they can escape.

Stoke have not exactly bounced back from their League Cup exit, which would have initially been filed under "well at least we can concentrate on the league." Stoke were battered by the Jekyll and Hyde team of the season, Everton. Ross Barkley was instrumental as Lukaku, Coleman and Lennon scored the goals. West Ham were beaten 1-0 by ten man Southampton who are really hitting form. Newcastle's 1-0 win over West Brom saw them sneak out of the relegation places. Swansea and Palace played out a 1-1 draw, little improvements from the team from Wales. Some Palace fans have taken to looking over their shoulders, could they plummet down the table?

14th February 2016

The increase in TV coverage of matches on a Sunday has often led to such days being called "Super" or "Special" or "Days of Destiny" or other such rubbish. However, Sunday could well have been a pivotal moment in the Premier League. The day started with leaders Leicester travelling to third placed Arsenal. Leicester led at half time, the mercurial Jamie Vardy "winning" and scoring a penalty on the stroke of half time. For anyone wondering about the inverted commas, let's just say that the front man didn't have to look too hard to find a leg to tumble over in the area. Leicester looked odds on to see off the Gunners and possibly kill of any dreams of a Wenger title. But no, things can change very quickly, especially if the referee decides to send off one of their defenders. Arsenal sprang to life and Walcott brought the scores level before Welbeck scored a shock winner deep into injury time. Randomly, it led me to think when the last time such an important top-of-the-table clash was settled by three English goal-scorers. Anyway, moving on!

A word in the ear of Joleon Lescott, if I may. When having just been battered 6-0 by Liverpool, a Liverpool that Paul Merson felt might have been there for the taking (which might explain Merson's management career), it would probably be wise not to tweet a picture of your new £150,000 car. Just saying Joleon, just saying. The fact that the car probably has a smaller turning circle than yourself nowadays has nothing to do with it. It is not even necessary to review the game. Villa were the Villa of a few months ago and Liverpool turned up.

Tottenham Hotspur, fresh with the knowledge that Leicester had slipped up, went to the Etihad to face-off with Manchester

City. A win would have seen Spurs glide back into second and close the gap to two points and a win for City would have got them right back in the thick of things. A Harry Kane penalty opened the scoring before City sub Iheanacho drew them level. Spurs drove on, and Dane Christian Eriksen fired home the kind of winner that suggests that Spurs might be the fairytale this season, as opposed to Leicester.

Before the early kick off on Saturday Louis Van Gaal claimed he would be "very unhappy" if United approached Mourinho behind his back. To be fair Louis, they've been doing it right in front of you so what say you of that, eh? Either way, losing 2-1 to Sunderland and admitting you will not get into the Champions League places is not exactly going to stop the Portuguese measuring up a few pictures in your office, is it? United were poor, Sunderland's new signings Kone and Khazri excelled and the Black Cats have a chance of survival.

Newcastle have been splashing the cash themselves, but seem to be determined to see how their new signings fare in the Championship. Chelsea, hardly the most attacking of teams in recent sides, put the Magpies to the sword turning them over 5-1 at the Bridge. Pedro was either choosing to play well to get a summer move, or maybe give the new manager an insight to what he used to play like, but either way his double and general performance was fundamental to Hiddink's biggest win since returning as caretaker.

Those Pardew for England rumours seem to have gone away, don't they? Palace are in their own mini freefall, this time losing 2-1 at home to Watford. Part one of Pardew's master plan worked, Adebayor notching his first for the club. Sadly for Palace, Deeney got a brace to send three points to Vicarage Road.

Norwich were in dreamland when Wes Hoolahan scored just eleven minutes after Robbie Brady to put them 2-0 up at home to West Ham. A lot can change in eleven minutes as it was exactly the same time that elapsed for the Hammers to score two of their own to leave Carrow Road with a point. Norwich are in desperate trouble, slipping nearer the trap door once again. Stoke put their recent troubles behind them, winning 3-1 at Bournemouth. Club record signing Imbula ended the goal drought after just nine minutes and Stoke did not need to look back. The defeat for Bournemouth has them looking over their shoulders and Stoke might just fancy a last push for a European place if they can string together a run of form.

Southampton are somewhat impregnable currently. Six games have now passed without the ball passing Fraser Forster. Six clean sheets have led to the Saints occupying 6th place and their 1-0 win over Swansea, albeit far from entertaining, was solid to say the least. Swansea still have relegation worries and will need to bounce back from this disappointment rapidly.

Leicester, Spurs or Arsenal? The answer seems to change weekly. I'm still going Leicester. Or Spurs. Not Arsenal, it's never Arsenal.

21st February 2016
Yes indeed folks, no Premier League action to be seen anywhere in this edition. We are all about the FA Cup and a

couple of European games from last week today. Let's start with Europe, shall we? Primarily because I have been bursting at the seams since Thursday to point at Manchester United and shake my head with disappointment.

Louis. It is pretty damn obvious that you are not going to qualify for the Champions League via the league route. I know you "would rather win the FA Cup than the Europa League" because you won the UEFA Cup at some point in your glittering career and would love to win something in England before they give you the heave-ho, but considering said Europa League is a route to playing Champions League football next season would it not have been wise to beat Midtjylland on Thursday night? I have a conspiracy theory. Louis knows his number is up, has heard via Inter Milan that Jose is definitely at Old Trafford next season and has decided to sabotage any chance of "The Special One" being in Europe's elite competition. I would love this to be true. United were terrible in Denmark but, realistically, have a chance of winning the second leg 1-0 and progressing. Just don't expect the goal to come early, hey? Who knows, by the time you read this Shrewsbury might have made all this chat irrelevant by knocking United out of the FA Cup on Monday night.

Liverpool and Spurs both played out draws away from home last Thursday, and Chelsea were beaten 2-1 in Paris on Wednesday night meaning that each tie is still firmly in the balance.

The last thing Arsenal really needed in their quest for the Premier League, Champions League and FA Cup treble (I know, it won't happen but still) was a 0-0 draw with Hull, meaning a replay to be played in a the next couple of weeks. Leicester, feet up and resting this weekend, would have been chuffed to bits to see the Hull goalkeeper make save after save to add another fixture into the already clogged list at the Emirates.

Everton might be sneakily fancying their chances of some silverware this season. Disappointing in the league and massively inconsistent used to be the recipe of a team you'd rather avoid drawing in the FA Cup, so a 2-0 win at Bournemouth will have raised the hopes at Goodison Park. After all, Martinez has won the FA Cup before whilst having a bad league season. Last season's semi-finalists Reading are eyeing up another potential trip down the M4 to Wembley. Brian McDermott's team came from a goal down to beat a full strength West Bromwich Albion 3-1 in a game that was marred by a coin thrown from the crowd striking Albion player Chris Brunt. Watford beat Leeds 1-0 at Vicarage Road, meaning their season still has some life in it with Premier League survival all but guaranteed.

Sunday saw the "box office" ties of the round. Chelsea, with a Dutchman in charge that needs not to win another trophy in England to flatter his ego, played Manchester City who seem somewhat determined to make it a little more challenging for Pep when he takes over in the summer. By challenging I mean completely lacking in the 2015/16 trophy department. I admit to not watching the game, but when I saw the following stat float across my social media timeline I had a feeling it might end up a home win. The shirt numbers of the eleven Manchester City players starting the match added up to over

440. Chelsea took the game a little more seriously, and got their just desserts winning 5-1.

As daft as this might sound, and who would have thought any comment in this column could ever be considered daft, the best thing that could have happened to Spurs this season was losing in the FA Cup. As luck would have it, Palace agreed. Pardew's men might have forgotten how to play Premier League football, but they could be considered another team worth avoiding in the draw. Leicester, still feet up on the sofa, would have preferred the result to go the other way but hey, you can't have everything.

Finally, a note to Blackburn Rovers. When playing a decent West Ham side, it probably helps if you keep eleven men on the pitch. Having someone stupidly sent off is not advisable and could lead to a 5-1 defeat.

The weekend concluded with the Quarter Final draw. Everton fans, full of the joys of spring a mere few paragraphs ago were left distraught when they drew Chelsea. Both Reading and Palace will be hopeful of progressing having drawn each other, where West Ham await Shrewsbury when they do away with United. Arsenal or Hull will play host to Watford. My picks for winners? Chelsea, Palace, West Ham and Watford. I really would not put money on it, but they would be nice semi-finals wouldn't they?

I am sure I tipped someone to win the FA Cup a few weeks ago, but for the life of me cannot remember who. Either way, they are probably out by now. Back to normal next week, if there is such a thing, as the Premier League resumes.

28th February 2016

At 17:40 on Saturday evening I was starting to tap away with my, "oh well Leicester, it was fun whilst it lasted" piece for this newspaper and then they went and changed it all again, didn't they? Two minutes later and I was having to start this column all over again. Oh Leicester, you little teases making us all think that you were going to fail to beat Norwich and let your title challenge disintegrate just like Walkers Crisps do in the sun. Time to give Ranieri a whole season's worth of credit, his substitution and injection of a little Ulloa led to the last minute winner from the Argentine. If Leicester pick up momentum again and close out this title I hope people remember that tactical change as a pivotal moment. What do I mean if? Of course they will.

"Will" became even more likely with the Sunday results. Two games is normally long enough to label someone the new "Rooney/Lineker/Owen/Fowler/Henry/Shearer/Charlton/Giggs/Best/Pele" so Marcus Rashford must be the new one of them, maybe even two of them rolled into one. Having come off the bench to save United's blushes in Europe (see Eurovision for more information) the young striker started against Arsenal. Graeme Souness, who played far better than he managed and managed far better than he pundits on Sky, suggested that Rashford might have been out of his depth against an Arsenal defence. Graeme, he was playing against Arsenal's defence! Rashford marked his first Premier League start with another double which led United to a 3-2 win against a team that seems unlikely to catch Leicester now. Face the truth Arsene, Chelsea, United and City have all gone backwards this season and you have still failed to win the title. Let someone else have a go next season.

All Spurs needed to do was keep winning, therefore applying subtle pressure to Leicester. Ranieri's boys will have sat with their feet up once again, revelling in the fact that both North London teams might slip up, and they nearly got their wish. Swansea led Tottenham for the majority of the game, but these Spurs players are made of stronger stuff than previous years. With twenty minutes to go they knuckled down and turned a 1-0 deficit into a 2-1 win.

The Saturday afternoon games were fairly dull, if truth be known. They had been preceded by West Ham beating Sunderland 1-0 in a game that was never likely to capture the imagination and the result leaves Sunderland in the relegation zone. Mind you, considering they have spent the vast majority of the season there this should not be the most surprising news of the weekend. Do you remember when some people were talking Stoke up to be the new Barcelona? Fools. Now they have slumped to a level so low that they can only manage to beat Villa 2-1. The shame of it all. Arnautovic got a brace to continue Villa's descent into Championship obscurity. Seriously, put some money on Villa winning League One in the 2017/18 season.

Poor Fraser Forster. Having just set a club record of 708 minutes without conceding a goal he completely forgot what he was in goal for and watched Fabregas' cross-cum-shot-cum-feeble-attempt-at-kicking-a-ball bobble into the corner. Clearly distraught and not used to seeing a number registered in the goals against column, big Fraser was unable to keep out Ivanovic's late header which sealed a surprise 2-1 win for Chelsea on the south coast. Whereas many of the Saturday afternoon kick offs started in a boring fashion and improved, Bournemouth and Watford started in a boring fashion and got worse, the game ending 0-0. With entertainment at a premium, you can imagine my personal joy at noticing the late televised game was WBA at home to Palace!

Mock not, mock not. The most nailed on 0-0 in recent Premier League history turned out to be a five goal thriller. WBA, clearly forgetting everything Pulis had said to them before kickoff, raced out of the blocks and led 3-0 at half time. Palace, clearly forgetting everything Pardew had said before kickoff and then suddenly remembering at half time, fought back superbly in the second period to make it 3-2. Cast your mind back to earlier in the season when I think I suggested Pardew might be a good shout for England manager. No league wins in ten games goes a long way to remind you that I know very little about this game. They couldn't end up getting dragged into the relegation mess, could they?

At the end of the weekend Leicester still lead the way, ahead of Spurs by two points. Arsenal have drifted to five points short of top place and City, well they had other things on their minds.

We end today's column with the first silverware of the season. No Arsene, the Community Shield did not count. Manchester City and Liverpool headed down the motorway to Wembley to contest the League Cup Final. Jurgen Klopp may well be one of the most likeable characters on British footballing shores currently, but hands up if you enjoyed the irony of a German manager seeing his team lose on penalties? No? Just me then! Actually, I fib. I would have loved to have seen Klopp lift a title so early in his Liverpool reign, but then by a similar token I was pleased to see Pellegrini at least win something since being told he was being Pepped. Caballero may have his critics, but he was rather good at stopping those penalties. Mignolet also has his critics. I have no idea why, he is fully deserving of a new five-year deal, isn't he Jurgen?

3rd March 2016
Those Leicester boys. They could fall head first into a well and come up with all the pennies that have been thrown down there. They played WBA on Tuesday night and were held to a 2-2 draw, to which came the cries of "that's all Spurs have been waiting for" and "that's the mistake Arsenal needed to see" and "it's too soon to completely write off City!" Wednesday night saw West Ham beat Spurs 1-0, Swansea beat Arsenal 2-1 at Arsenal and Liverpool batter City 3-0 at Anfield. What say you to all that then?

From looking likely to drop behind Spurs on goal difference Leicester led the way on Thursday morning by three points. This was the first time Spurs played under the spotlight of potentially going top of the pile and the least Spurs like side of recent years played exactly like the kind of Spurs team everyone has got used to in the last couple of decades. Spurs looked tired and West Ham were playing at full throttle and it was far from a happy birthday for the Poch. Still, Spurs still have a chance which is more than can be said for Arsenal.

Swansea's manager, Guidolin, missed the game after being rushed to hospital. Arsenal's entire squad missed the game because, let's be honest, they don't know how to win the games that really matter in the league. To make matters even worse, if possible, Cech was ruled out of the North London derby on Saturday as he injured himself racing back to his goal having gone forward for an injury time corner. Nothing smacks of desperation more than that last sentence!

Liverpool put in the sort of performance that gets you wondering what damage King Klopp might be able to do in the Premier League next season if given the tools required to improve the squad. City, possibly still celebrating the huge achievement of winning the League Cup at the weekend, were also on the same missing list as Arsenal as Liverpool romped to a 3-0 win, a win that allowed United to draw level on points with City. Imagine if United, lambasted all season from all quarters, pipped City to fourth spot and Pep was not in the Champions League next season.

Following some almost entertaining football at Old Trafford in the last couple of games, normal service was very much resumed against Watford. Rashford started once more and was joined by another 18-year-old in Fosu-Mensah. Both were impressive again, but it was left to Juan Mata to steal all three points with seven minutes remaining. As previously mentioned, this moved United level on points with City, albeit City having a game in hand.

Tuesday night's matches had an impact on Wednesday night's at both ends of the table. Sunderland fought back to grab a point at home to Palace. Norwich continued their nosedive towards relegation by losing at home to Chelsea, who must now be pretty confident in their own ability to avoid the drop. Villa managed to score, hurrah, but also managed to concede three at home to Everton and Bournemouth turned over

Southampton 2-0 in some kind of South Coast derby. Sunderland's point clawed them above Norwich and out of the drop zone, and with Swansea beating Arsenal it meant Newcastle could really, really not afford to lose at Stoke. Oh. Shaqiri condemned Steve Mc to yet another defeat. In the last calendar year, McLaren has one of the worst records in England for someone that has held a job in the last calendar year. Hey, I don't just make these stats up you know. Sunderland, Norwich and Newcastle all entered the weekend's games sitting on 24 points, and a mere four goals separating them on goal difference. Tight is the word you are looking for.

7th March 2016

That Claudio Ranieri. He must have put some kind of spell on the teams around Leicester City. Tuesday night, as you will have learned from reading the midweek special, saw Leicester drop two points against WBA. No bother, Claudio had already mystically arranged for Spurs, City and Arsenal to lose! The North London derby was the early kick off on Saturday and there was only one result that would really suit Leicester down to the ground. Claudio likes entertainment, so he would never have wished for a 0-0. No, the suave Italian is much more of an end to end 2-2 kind of guy when dishing out treats to the public, and maybe throw a red card in there too hey Claudio? Arsenal led, and then Coquelin was shown a second yellow card. His first was probably harsh, considering he had been fouled first, but Claudio's spell said drama. Alderweireld equalise and then Harry Kane scored a beauty to send Tottenham top of the league. But no, wait! Arsenal finally found a little bit of that bottle they had misplaced in the last fortnight to steal an equaliser. Sanchez netted his first league goal since October to give the Leicester fans what they wanted.

A point was great for the Foxes, but they still had to end Saturday's matches with their own right result. Now would not be a good time for teams to have worked out how to stop the Leicester juggernaut and for the third game running it looked like the leaders might struggle to find the win. Without stating the obvious, to win the title you need match winners when it is going against you and Leicester have one very special talent in Riyad Mahrez. Ten minutes into the second half the ball fell to him on the edge of the area. A lesser player, say Rooney for example, would have thumped it first time. Mahrez brought it under, shimmied in a way that you would only see on Strictly and then curled it delightfully into the top corner. That was all they needed to go five points clear.

Of course, the Premier League is not just about Leicester no matter how much I talk about them. There are a few other teams in certain predicaments that need a mention. How about Villa? That will cheer a few people up. Many people were left tearing their betting slips up in a rage following Villa's 4-0 defeat to City. In a rage, you ask? Yes, as most people will have bet on City winning by at least six! The win for City puts them in reach of Arsenal if they win their game in hand.

Will Steve McLaren still have a job by the time you read this? Newcastle's manager/director was on the receiving end of a 3-1 drubbing by Bournemouth followed by some choice words from the majority of the St James Park faithful. Mike

Ashley must be working out whether to stick or twist with the club sitting second bottom with a game in hand. The caveat is that winning the game in hand would see them move out of the relegation zone. Norwich are in even worse form than Newcastle, losing 1-0 to Swansea. The victory for Swansea, like Bournemouth, was another huge step to safety with the gap now being eight points with nine to play. Sunderland must have felt they had earned a huge three points away to Southampton before the magnificently named Virgil van Dijk thumped home a late leveller. The single point sees Sunderland sit marginally above the drop zone.

If you want value for money, go and watch Everton play. 2-0 up, even with ten men after Mirallis was sent off, should normally be enough for most teams to guarantee a win. Not Everton, oh no. They wanted to give Slaven Bilic a happy memory in his first dugout return to the club he played for, letting West Ham battle their way back (and I use battle in its loosest sense) to a 3-2 victory. The Hammers sit fifth, a mere point behind City.

Chelsea are apparently unbeaten in the league under Guus. A 1-1 draw with Stoke continued that run and saw the Champions finally appear in the top half of the table.

Here's a little fun fact for you. On Christmas Day, Crystal Palace were level on points with the top four. Now they are level on points with Swansea. They are falling faster than Christian Benteke did under a Damian Delaney challenge in injury time. Pardew says he dived, but Delaney gave him the option of hitting the deck. Benteke got up as quickly as he fell over to score the penalty and give Liverpool their first win at Selhurst Park since 1993.

If you get a chance, watch Juan Mata pick up two yellow cards against WBA. There were just 158 seconds between the two, and both were pretty foolish. Twenty six minutes had been played when Mata decided he would rather watch the somewhat underwhelming 1-0 defeat from the bench. Who can blame him, United are scintillating to watch and WBA are the West Country Barcelona at times. Rondon got the only goal in a 1-0 win for WBA, a win that cut short the "Manchester United might just end up in the Champions League places" revival.

14th March 2016
Is it just me, or are revivals in football getting shorter and shorter?

Take Chelsea for example. They were at a revival factor of seven and a half after going unbeaten in the Premier League since Guus came in to steady the ship. However, following their fairly empty departure from the Champions League against PSG and then Saturday's exit from the FA Cup, one would presume that revival factor has dropped significantly. Manchester United, having won some games and even scored some goals looked as though their revival might have peaked at factor eight. However, the defeat at WBA was followed up by one of the worst United performances of recent memory (and there has been some stiff competition for that accolade this season) in a 2-0 Europa League loss at Liverpool. Spurs were in the opposite of a revival, so revival factor minus three having lost to West Ham, drawn with Arsenal and been given a Europa League lesson in football Dortmund style. Dortmund, previously managed by Jurgen Klopp, won comfortably 3-0. Whom do you need to play to restart a revival? Aston Villa of course! Spurs duly thumped them 2-0, Harry Kane helping himself to a couple of goals.

This whole revival thing begs a few questions. Are Palace in revival now they are in the FA Cup Semi Final? Their 2-0 win over Reading, no matter how late they left it, could be seen as the spark to turning their league form around. For every person that thinks that, be sure to remember Wigan a few seasons ago. Cup winners and relegated in the same season. Not that I think Palace will be relegated, but they do need to win a league game at some point.

If I know Rafa Benitez, which I don't incidentally, he will be reading this column and be most miffed that it has taken to the fourth paragraph for his return to the Premier League to get a mention. I tell you what Rafa, you thought managing the egos of Real Madrid was difficult? Try this lot at St James Park. The worst kept secret of the week was McLaren keeping his Newcastle gig whilst Ashley's minions went to see if they could talk Benitez into replacing him. They didn't have to try too hard, Rafa was already walking from Merseyside to Tyneside when they found him by the side of the motorway sipping some water and explaining to the passing cars why it is very important to have seven defensive players on the pitch. If Rafa keeps them up he wins a three year deal. That is a very big if. By the time you read this, Rafa will have realised how big his task is having taken a beating by Leicester. Or Rafa will be the new Tyneside messiah having beaten the league leaders. Either way.

Bournemouth must be safe now. On the south coast Eddie Howe's boys came off the sunny side up in a five-goal thriller, beating Swansea. Swansea manager, Guidolin, has recently been in hospital with heart trouble. Having seen his side come from a goal behind twice, only to lose, would suggest that the outpatients department might have had a visitor Sunday morning. Stoke and Southampton ended in a Southampton win.

Roberto Martinez likes the FA Cup, having won it already in his career. He likes it even more now as Roman Lukaku finally scored against his old club to see the Toffees through to the semi finals. Both teams ended with ten men. Diego Costa, equally unbelievably as expectedly, saw red for only the second time in his career and Gareth Barry got two yellows for the Merseyside team. There was talk that Costa might have had a nibble on Barry Suarez style, though Everton were keen to play that down after the game. This made PSG's midweek tweet, calling Costa a fraud, finally make sense. Because you only get 180 characters on Twitter the tweet meant to say "Diego Costa models himself on Luis Suarez, but he is a fraud. I mean, he hasn't even bitten anyone!"

Louis van Gaal has said many times that he would rather win the FA Cup than the Europa League, words that must have still been ringing in the ears of his players at Anfield on Thursday night. United played West Ham on Sunday and they needed Martial to cancel out Payer's wonder strike for the visitors. This was the only quarter final to need a replay, which won't bother United too much as they are likely to have midweek's free quite soon.

Arsenal fans were talking a lot about how special winning the FA Cup three times in a row would be. If you fell into their trap, you'd have ended up believing that it was better than winning the Premier League, Champions League and the World Cup all in the same season. Therefore, their quarter final with Watford had to be one of the biggest games in the famous old club's history, surely? We all know how Arsenal perform when the pressure is on. In one of the most nailed on sending's off since Cameroon played Argentina in Italia '90, Arsenal's Gabriel saw red for removing Deeney's legs from his body. Ighalo, without a goal for a fair while, ended that drought to give Watford the lead and Guedioura unleashed a thunderbolt that nearly took the net off to make it two. Welbeck pulled one back very late before missing an injury time sitter that put paid to any hopes of a historic feat.

I have a new theory on Manchester City. It goes like this. Aguero got all the boys in the dressing room and suggested something like "look lads, Pep is going to get rid of all of us this summer. Even me, and I am way better than all of you (looking at Yaya Toure in particular when he said that bit). Here's my idea. Let's be rubbish for the rest of the season so that all his new players don't get to play in the Champions League next year!" No? How else could City draw 0-0 with Norwich? The real test of my theory will come in the match at the Etihad midweek, where City will look to defend their first leg lead against Kyiv. If they lose that, then that conversation definitely happened.

21st March 2016
In years gone by this would be the time of year that United would steadily move through the gears, chase down anyone that had dared gone ahead of them in the table and invariably end up breaking some hearts. Well Louis, just pretend that the top three don't exist and you might be able to play that game yourself whilst adopting a thick Scottish accent and pointing at your watch a lot. United beat City in the Manchester derby with a goal from young Marcus Rashford, who according to many should now be on the plane to Euro 16. They boy striker now has five goals in his first eight United matches. Rashford became the youngest goalscorer in a Premier League Manchester derby in a stat that once again reminds us of the television's desire to brain wash us into thinking football started in 1992. It took Cantona ten games to score his first five and Van Nistelrooy thirteen. That's it, Rashford is definitely the next kid on the "wasn't he supposed to be the next Michael Owen" block. The win keeps United in sixth, but closes the gap on City in fourth to a mere point.

West Ham are the meat in the Manchester sandwich, having drawn 2-2 at Chelsea following a somewhat dubious late penalty given to the hosts. Fabregas scored it to gain the nearly-former-Champions a point. The Hammers have the same points as United, but are one goal to the good. Just imagine if they see off both City and United and finish fourth themselves. All that taxpayers money will have gone to good use if Champions League football is welcomed at the Olympic Stadium in its first year. Take that Leyton Orient, hey?

Leicester, fresh from seeing off a much improved Newcastle 1-0 last Monday, saw off a much improved but still incapable of winning Crystal Palace by the same score line. Mahrez added yet another goal to his tally to momentarily send Leicester eight points clear with seven games remaining. Eight points became five by the end of the weekend, Spurs making very light work of Bournemouth. Harry Kane and Delle Alli inspired them to a comfortable 3-0 win. Whilst I am on the subject of Kane and Alli, and Jamie Vardy and Danny Drinkwater for that matter, if they do not feature in the England team this summer then there is something very, very wrong in football. Four English players playing at the absolute top of their game in teams that are fighting for the title. I can almost guarantee that this summer's eleven will feature out of form "stars" such as Sterling, Rooney, Lallana and Delph. Not that Delph is a star, he might need to let Pep know who he is when the Spaniard arrives.

Sunday afternoon also saw interesting conversation directional changes at half time at St Mary's. "That Klopp, he is getting Liverpool firing now, isn't he?" Liverpool led Southampton 2-0 and were very good value for their lead. Southampton, traditionally Liverpool's feeder team, were just messing about for the first forty five minutes and decided to put in a late shift. Incredibly the game ended 3-2 to the Saints.

If there was one team in the league who needed a win more than Palace, it was Norwich. Their match with WBA was never likely to win "most glamorous game of the weekend" but it was a huge three points for the team from Norfolk. To make their weekend even better, Sunderland and Newcastle played out a tempestuous 1-1 draw that did neither team any good whatsoever.

Jekyll and Hyde's favourite team Everton would have fancied their chances against an Arsenal side that seem to still believe there is some mileage left in their title challenge. Arsenal gave their fans further false hope with an impressive 2-0 win. Everton's minds were probably in the same location as Watford's, the location marked "FA Cup Semi Final coming up soon." Watford fell to a 2-1 defeat against Stoke.

Swansea eased further away from the relegation mire, beating everybody's favourite team to play when needing points, Aston Villa. By the time you read this, Villa might be on the verge of another mission impossible. Remi Garde is rumoured to be on the verge of having his dream come true, an early sacking from a job he was mad to take in the first place. Don't worry Remi, in six months time when Villa lose at Rotherham they won't even remember your name.

27th March 2016
Regular readers of this column will know how I can barely contain my excitement as international weekends rock around. What finer way to spend an Easter weekend than watching teams such as England put out weakened teams and slip two goals behind the world champions, right?

It is fair to say I have grown a little weary of Roy Hodgson and the tactics that served him quite well a few decades back. Worryingly I was one of the very few that felt he was a better appointment than the Jordan manager a few years ago. I was virtually apoplectic that Danny Welbeck was selected ahead of Jamie Vardy, vowing to care even less about the England side than in recent times. Toni Kroos and Mario Gomez moving

Germany into a two-nil lead before the hour was more than vindicating my view point.

If you cannot celebrate turning a 2-0 deficit against the World Champions into a 3-2 victory, albeit in a friendly, when can you? To make it even better, three stars of the New Top Order got the goals. First, Harry Kane drilled in to give England a sniff and then Jamie Vardy rose from the bench to make it all square. Kane's goal was a classic moment of calm in a crowded area. The ball arrived to him from a corner, yet he was facing the wrong way. With a move the late Johan Cruyff would have been proud of Kane twisted round and got his shot away in an instant, nestling low in the far corner of the German net. Not to be outdone, substitute Vardy raised the bar. Clyne raced down the right once again and his cross was a fraction behind the darting run of the Leicester forward. Yet Vardy is a man full of confidence and a slightly misplaced cross is not something to get him worried these days. He simply caught the ball on the half volley behind his standing leg and watched it fly home. When you are the main marksman of the Premier League leaders, this is all in a day's work. Let's be honest, Roy would have taken that wouldn't he? His experimental team had fought back admirably, but no. Seize the Dier! Germany will have been a touch disappointed in the manner they conceded the injury time winner from the Tottenham midfielder. Henderson put in a simple near post corner where Dier rose unchallenged to power the ball home with a fine header. That's it, England will now win Euro 2016, right? It was also very nice to see the smile on Gary Neville's face as he remembered how nice it is to win a game of football.

Let us not get too carried away. Unleashing the likes of Kane, Vardy and the superb Dele Alli in a friendly is one thing. Having the strength of mind to select them ahead of long term favourites like Rooney, Wilshere (yes Roy has intimated that he will select Wilshere regardless of any match minutes, purely a fitness test) and Welbeck in the heat of a major championships is another. That said, Roy picked quite the experimental side against Germany and hopefully some players played themselves into those absolutely garish new shirts that have been released. Don't let us down Roy, if we are going to fail let us fail they way we want, awful shirts and all. Plus, let's see how we do on Tuesday night shall we?

Following the sad news that football revolutionary Johan Cruyff had passed away earlier in the week, the friendly match between the Netherlands and France was momentarily paused after 14 minutes as a mark of respect to the first European football superstar. The game ended in a 3-2 win for France, with Dimi Payet impressing for Deschamps' men. There has been a great deal said and written about the Dutch legend in the last seven days. Nothing I say now will be that original, but for me football might have looked completely different without Johan Cruyff. No Cruyff would have meant Holland would not be seen as the country of the football hipster. Barcelona would be completely different today if it were not for Cruyff, for it was he that instigated the philosophy that Guardiola carried on and the La Masia academy that gave the world Xavi, Iniesta and Leo Messi. Just imagine, if Cruyff had not spotted a slow right winger and turned him into a metronomic central midfielder that could deliver his tactical wishes, Pep Guardiola would have been lost to football. If Cruyff hadn't built Ajax as a football power, then we would never have had Louis Van Gaal. Actually United fans, just ponder that one for a while.

Ronaldo missed a penalty in a surprise 1-0 defeat for Portugal against Bulgaria. The Republic of Ireland got an impressive win at home to Switzerland whilst Wales and Northern Ireland sized each other up and shook hands on a 1-1 draw. Scotland, about five months too late, put it all together and beat the Czech Republic 1-0, something that is bound to keep them warm at night as they watch Euro 2016 on the television.

2nd April 2016

I know, I know, two international round-up's in two weeks! You might start thinking I care about international football. Anyway, I thought today we would look a little bit into some of the results of the second round of friendlies and see what they might mean, if anything at all, for some of the nations.

England 1 – 2 Holland

That "England to win Euro 2016" bandwagon barely got out of the station, hey? Key points from this game include Danny Rose not quite being Roberto Carlos yet. England have been crying out for a defender that can play a bit since Bobby Moore and one comes along and the media try to kill him off. Damn you John Stones for slipping over on a slippery surface. Let the kid play, even if it means making a mistake or two. Finally, can someone show me exactly where the Rooney shaped hole is in the team that he is expected to fill? I cannot see it for the life of me. We have a young squad that is capable of pressing, moving the ball at a high tempo and basically play some high energy attacking football. They are all playing this style for their clubs thanks to the likes of Pochettino, Ranieri and Martinez. Or, we could pick Rooney in the eleven who does not have the physical capability to play in that style of game and is playing for the slowest, most one-tempoed team in the Premier League. Come on Roy, even you can work this one out. Oh, and despite a strong dislike for him, John Terry would be a decent shout to play on the left side of the central pair, if you put Stones next to him. Holland, well they must be gutted they are not playing this summer.

France 4 – 2 Russia
Watch out for this French team. The last time they hosted a major championships they won it. Even without the Real Madrid troublemaker Benzema they have quite the range of attacking options. Kante, scoring on his birthday, must have secured a place in Deschamps midfield. Payet also starred in his cameo and would not be a bad player to bring off the bench for any of the teams who have qualified.

Germany 4 – 1 Italy
Standard Italian fare this. Shocking form before the tournament, tick. Scandal and grumbles in Italian football before the tournament, tick (in this case the Italian media being offended that Conte is about to do one to Chelsea and not respecting the Azzurri). Get to the final of the tournament, probable tick. Do not be fooled by this result. They played well against Spain and were facing a German side that had a rocket up them from Low for sinking as low as losing to England. Conte is one of the most intense coaches in the modern game, and there is no way he will be panicking and there is no way he will allow his players to slacken off in the knowledge their coach is leaving soon.

Portugal 2 – 1 Belgium
Hang on, weren't this Belgium team supposed to be one of the greatest European teams ever? Portugal, fresh from losing to Bulgaria, were never in real danger against their opponents. This is probably the last chance for this Belgian side to reach the heights they were expected to scale. But surely any team with Lukaku, Courtois, Hazard, De Bruyne and, erm, Felliani should do well?

Republic of Ireland 2 – 2 Slovakia
Nobody is expecting Ireland to do anything great in the summer and their task has got harder in the knowledge that they might have to turn to Shay Given following Rob Elliot's heartbreaking injury. Also without Chris Brunt, the Irish will probably hoping not to get too outclassed. Still, if they keep picking up cheap penalties then who knows.

Northern Ireland 1 – 0 Slovenia
The lads from the North, and St Ives, are unbeaten in ten games. Yes, count them. Ten. It would be incredible if they continue that form much longer, but they might cause a few teams some problems in France. A lot will still come down to whether Kyle Lafferty gets fit in time, but if they keep finding people like Washington to score goals then they could surprise a few folks.

Ukraine 1 – 0 Wales
If you take the apples out of an apple pie, what are you left with? A lot of crumbly pastry. Wales did not have Bale or Ramsey for this international weekend. I will let you work out the analogy for yourselves.

Scotland 1 – 0 Denmark
I would hate to be a Scottish fan at the moment, it must be hell. Two very respectable 1-0 wins against two better sides than they in a row would normally be cause for hope, if not celebration. The only problem? Both wins have come a few games too late for the Scots. If they could have mustered anything like this at the back end of qualification then there could have been party in France involving some kilts.

3rd April 2016
Let's get the elephant out of the room shall we? This whole "Premier League clubs might have been doping" thing that broke over the weekend. Arsenal fans, if this is genuinely your best hope of winning the title now then you probably need to have a chat with yourselves. I pick on Arsenal as social media was awash with deluded fans hoping that everyone other than them might be getting a slap on the wrist. For a brief moment there was talk of a points deduction, of players being banned. But hey, never let the facts get in the way of false hope. Dr Bonar, investigated by the English paper The Sunday Times, allegedly prescribed banned substances to elite British sports people as recently as two years ago. Leicester, Chelsea and even Arsenal were mentioned. Yes, Arsenal. The fans on social media probably missed that bit. However, The Sunday Times also said it have very little evidence to support the allegation. I am not naive enough to believe that all this match fixing, drug taking and anything corrupt happens anywhere than in the Premier League, but it would be a crying shame for one of the most thrilling title races in decades to be overshadowed by unsubstantiated

claims. That's the dull stuff out of the way, shall we crack on with the bit we all care about?

Leicester are still running away with the damn thing! Twelve points from their remaining six games guarantees them the most unlikely of titles having beaten Southampton, you guessed it, 1-0 on Sunday. Efficient is the word you are looking for, and supporters of Nottingham Forest are still trying to work out how a team with Wes Morgan as their skipper are going to win the league. I don't know Forest fans, maybe a good manager and better players around him has brought the best out of Wes? It was the head of the central defender that thumped the ball past Fraser Forster late in the first half and even the most hopeful of Spurs fan knew that was another three points in the Foxes' bag.

Spurs missed their chance on Saturday night at Anfield, where they needed a Harry Kane equaliser to leave with a point. That opened to door wide open once again for Ranieri's men and, to be blunt, they rarely miss an opportunity to turn the screw and the gap became seven points. Let's be candid, if this was a Manchester United side of the 90's winning games 1-0, the title would not be in doubt. Equally, there is no conceivable reason why Leicester will not see this most remarkable of seasons out.

It is equally inconceivable that Newcastle will recover from the bitter mental blow they took at Norwich on Saturday afternoon. 1-0 down, Mitrovic equalised for the Magpies. They instantly conceded, you know, just to make it a bit more nerve racking for the fans. There was mass jubilation when a penalty was awarded and Mitrovic calmly slotted it away for

2-2. A point would have been great for Benitez at this point, which Sunderland labouring to another draw. But no, this is Newcastle United isn't it. Why do it the easy way? Martin Olsson popped up to give Norwich an injury time winner that sent Carrow Road berserk and opened up the gap between Alex Neill's men and their fellow relegation battlers to four points. Sunderland and Newcastle, it has to be said, do have a game in hand.

Crystal Palace are still looking nervously over their shoulders following a somewhat fortunate 2-2 draw with West Ham. Palace must have been delighted to find the net twice in the same game, but the Hammers were furious at a shocking red card being handed out to Kouyate. It is all well and good that the ban will be rescinded, one would imagine, but when Bilic's men are doing all they can to make it the most unlikely top four in Premier League history they could do without idiotic refereeing.

With United winning 1-0 at home to Everton the Hammers trail Van Gaal's men by two points and City by three. King Louis further endeared himself to his boss before the game, saying he felt that United's proposed pre-season tour of China was "far from an ideal preparation for a season." I guess that depends which side of the fence you sit Louis, Ed Woodward may well have an official partner for Chinese Noodles up his sleeve. Martial scored United's 1000th Old Trafford Premier League goal in the win, a target they have been slowly chipping away at one shot per week at a time.

Manchester City and Arsenal both frustrated their supporters even further, putting Bournemouth and Watford to bed respectively, 4-0. For City it smacked of playing when they can be bothered and for Bournemouth it smelled of a team that know they are safe. For Arsenal it looked a little bit like doing what they always do, clinical performances when it matters least. Watford were running around in their Cup Semi Final suits, so it was quite obvious where their minds were.

No Tales from the Top Flight would be complete with some thoughts on Aston Villa. Remi Garde was put out of his misery earlier in the week when everybody realised that it would have been hard enough to save Villa if he had £50m to spend, let alone asking him to do it with nothing. In a rare moment of sense, it looks like Villa have decided to wait to the summer to try and convince someone it is a job worth taking and have switched their attention to collecting former FA executives to sit at the board table instead. Oh, and Brian Little. Because bringing back a club legend is the way the reconnect the club to the fans apparently. Personally, I prefer the not losing to Chelsea 4-0 approach. The fans might appreciate that a little more. Guus Hiddink went all experimental in his selection and would have been quite pleased at what he saw, until he remembered he was playing a team that would struggle to survive in the Championship right now.

Neither Stoke or Swansea will have been that bothered that their game ended 2-2. Stoke don't want to win anymore as that might mean ending up in the Europa League and Swansea are safe so everyone went home happy.

I'm really in an Arsenal baiting kind of mood today. With the PFA team of the year due to be announced very soon I can well imagine Ozil, who has been excellent this year, being selected. This is bound to be followed with Arsenal fans moaning that he has been picked out of position and that Wenger should go. Just remember folks, you had Bruce Rioch before Arsene.

17th April 2016

As a famous Scot once said, "Football, eh?" Whereas my "Your Week in Sport" cup is half empty, this column's cup is positively overflowing. Where on earth do I start?

Manchester City! Two shocks in that game. No, not Ibra bottling the big occasion again. Firstly the 1-0 against PSG meaning City are through to the semi finals. Did anyone actually see that coming? Now now, don't pretend. We all had that down as another early exit for the Citizens. Despite being the team everyone wanted to draw in the semi finals, Real Madrid had the greatest cause for celebration by seeing the two sides pulled out of the same hat in a fashion that will have suited Zidane. The second shock? Otamendi and Mangala actually looked like they had played football together before. I certainly didn't see that one coming either.

Not wishing to totally blur the lines between the Premier League and the Champions League, but wouldn't it be great to see Pellegrini knock out the club who sacked him after their record La Liga points haul then go on to beat Pep and Bayern in the final? Yes, that Pep who has been recruited to replace Pellegrini and win the elusive Champions League. It won't happen, but let us pretend that it might, even if only for the next five minutes. Madrid have got all Champions League greedy by having both teams in the semi finals. Atletico beat

Barcelona and Real came back from 2-0 down to wave off Wolfsburg.

King Klopp has a plan. That plan involves Champions League football next season at Anfield. It would have been too easy for Jurgen to secure it via the traditional method of 4th place in the league. Jurgen doesn't do simple, it is not cool enough. No, Jurgen plans to bring Champions League football to Anfield by winning the Europa League! At 2-0 down, then 3-1 down, not even the most fervent King Klopp devotee could have seen this plan still having legs come Friday morning. There was a reason earlier in the season Klopp had a pop at Liverpool fans leaving before the final whistle. Oh yes. Dejan Lovren headed home the winning goal in the fourth minute of injury time to seal a memorable comeback that saw many people dust off their "Istanbul" folders and trot out many a similarity. From 3-1 down with twenty minutes or so to go, Liverpool triumphed 4-3 and have been rewarded with a trip to Villareal. Just imagine if you had left that game at 3-1 down.

All this football chat and we have not gone near the Premier League yet.

Monday night's referee for the Tottenham match was changed after it emerged that Kevin Friend was a Leicester fan. Nobody was suggesting that Friend would have favoured Stoke in Monday's game, but it was felt it would be wise to remove any doubt by appointing. It later turned out Friend merely lives in Leicester and is a Bristol City fan, poor guy. After 90 minutes of the Leicester game on Sunday afternoon you could have thought Jonathan Moss was a Spurs fan following some of the most ludicrous decisions seen in a Premier League for at least a month. Leicester led through Vardy at half time. Before the half, Vardy picked up a disputable yellow for tracking back and catching his man. Minimal contact was made, but these things sometimes get a booking. On the hour, Vardy went chasing through into the West Ham area and there was a slight tangle in the box. Further viewing would suggest it was not a penalty, but to call Vardy out for allegedly diving was a very brave, if not interesting, call. Vardy received a second yellow for falling over after contact, Leicester being asked to play the remainder of the game with ten men. This was not an Ashley Young style dive to say the least, but hey Moss was merely warming up. Go and watch any professional match and see what happens at every corner in every match. Defenders grapple strikers, strikers grapple defenders. To decide who begins first is nigh on impossible. Moss decided that Morgan was grappling first on one occasion and gave the Hammers a hotly disputed penalty. If you give that, you have to give it every time, in every match. Carroll scored to make it 1-1 with eight minutes left. Leicester rocked, and Cresswell scored a lovely volley to make it 2-1. The drama was not over. Moss decided a replica situation with Huth being manhandled at a Leicester corner was not worthy of a penalty but, four minutes into time added on at the end, felt Schlupp tumbling under a Carroll "challenge" was. Ochoa showed nerves of steel to snatch a point for Leicester. If that had been Sunday League, you could have been forgiven for thinking that Moss had given Leicester one to make up for his mistakes. The point gained by Leicester was possibly not as important as the show of mental strength to fight back and get a draw. The gap opened up to eight points, with Spurs due to play before you read this.

Now I have got that out of my system we can talk relegation battles. I am fairly certain I called the relegation battle done and dusted last weekend after Newcastle capitulated at Southampton, Sunderland failed to win and Norwich managed to lose at Palace. When was I ever right? Sunderland sprung into life on Saturday lunchtime and destroyed Norwich's confidence with a 3-0 away win. Big Sam, he knows what to do at this time of year. Defoe was a constant menace and scored the all important second goal. Take that Newcastle! Benitez, having called out his players for a lack of mental strength in the week, must have been delighted in a very understated Rafa type way with their own 3-0 win over Swansea. It was Rafa's 56th birthday, so no doubt he spent the celebratory evening on the phone to Andros Townsend telling him that he needs to track back a little more often. The former Spurs wideman was excellent in the win, scoring the game's best goal and creating the other two. Swansea kind of knew they were safe, however.

Here is a glimpse of how inconsistent United are this season. Excellent in their midweek FA Cup win at West Ham which secured a semi final place against Everton, they laboured to a 1-0 win against Villa. The star of both shows was again Marcus Rashford, who stuck the literal two fingers up at Van Gaal who had attempted to make him the scapegoat of the previous loss at Tottenham. Rashford's goal at Upton Park was excellent, his goal against Villa slightly less so. The highlights of the match were really delivered by the Villa fans displaying excellent gallows humour with their songs, the best of which being "Joleon Lescott, he has a new car."

Everton fans are not stupid. They are not falling for the ruse that an FA Cup Semi Final means they have had a good season. Oh no. Bobby Martinez can praise his players all he wants in the press, but the Everton fans are somewhat old fashioned. They prefer to see them win on the pitch. To be fair, if Everton amassed points in line with the praise their garner from their manager, they would be challenging Leicester themselves. A 1-1 draw with Southampton is not to be sniffed at in this day and age, but the knives are out for Martinez and someone is looking for the sharpener.

One of my favourite weekend pastimes is watching Arsene Wenger. The Arsenal manager is a legend, but it is great fun to watch him talk up his side's involvement in the title race. Arsene. There is no title race involving your team sir. Even if you held on to the 1-0 lead against Palace, you were not in it. You are definitely not in it now you let Palace leave with a point, courtesy of Bolasie.

We finish today's column where we started. Manchester City. It's almost as if the players have decided they fancy playing for their incoming manager next season, and realised that if they play quite well now they stand a better chance than if they continued playing as if they really were not that bothered. Had they been bothered a little more often this whole season's story might have been completely different. Another hat-trick for Aguero means he has thirteen in his last twelve outings.

With matches being played midweek, I'm already looking forward to the next twist in the tale.

22nd April 2016

Watch out Leicester, Spurs are out to hunt you down. That was the clear message from Harry Kane with his "cheeky little Instagram" picture of lions (Spurs) waiting for their prey (Leicester). I am presuming that the lions in the picture were not faced with the prospect of some prey who have shut up shop for the summer, packed their flip flops and are already in the queue at East Midlands Airport to check in for their end of season jaunt to Dubai, for this is what faced Tottenham in the form of Stoke City. Two goals apiece for the excellent Kane and Alli saw that the gap at the top was reduced once again, and with time running out it seems that Spurs have no intention of slipping away any more quietly than Vardy leaving a football pitch having been shown a second yellow card. Or something like that.

Is this the season where Rafa Benitez starts out as a surprise choice for the Madrid job and ends up a surprise choice for the Newcastle job, but turns out to be the 2016 version of Kevin Keegan? I don't know if I can push the Keegan thing any further other than to say that the Geordie fans quite like him right now, but Rafa seems to be giving Newcastle some life about thirty minutes after they were very much pronounced dead at St Mary's. Since the Southampton show Newcastle have perked up somewhat, Vernon Anita scoring a cracking goal from right back of all places to take a point against an in-form Manchester City.

There is nothing like heading into an FA Cup Semi Final with a bit of form behind you and Everton, Palace and Watford headed into their weekend FA Cup Semi Finals with nothing like any form behind them. West Ham saw off Watford 3-1, without so much breaking a sweat. Credit for Watford's manager Flores however. Clearly struggling to find a way Gomes could practice saving penalties in recent weeks, he must have instructed his side to concede them in every game. With the chance that the Semi Final with Palace might go to spot kicks, Gomes has now faced four penalties in his last two games. Sadly for him, Mark Noble dispatched both comfortably to sit nicely alongside Andy Carroll's goal. That's nice for them both, it'll give them something to reminisce over when they spend their summer on holiday together, rather than being involved in Roy's England squad.

Bobby Martinez knows how much the Merseyside derby "means to it's fans" but he must have forgotten to pass on this wisdom to his players. Everton collapsed to a 4-0 defeat against their city rivals, who could not have believed their luck. One interesting point came out of the game, which is one more than Everton achieved. How is James Milner so excellent at crossing and so terrible at corners? Milner assisted both Origi and Sahko, the ball coming back to him after a poor corner to be redelivered with stunning accuracy. Funes Mori did not make it any easier for the Blues, getting a straight red for a shocking tackle on the inform Origi. I tell you what Bobby, if you are trying to get the Everton fans back on side, losing 4-0 to Liverpool is not the best way to do it. Maybe the FA Cup will save him?

If United against Palace turns out to be this year's FA Cup Final I hope to the skies that it is a better game than the one served up at Old Trafford. United actually scored in the first half, something as rare as a frenetic, attacking performance by

Van Gaal's men. Except they didn't actually score it, Damian Delaney turned Darmian's cross into his own net. It is saying something when your left back turns out to be your greatest attacking threat, as the Italian scored one of his own in the second half to seal a 2-0 win. Of the three semi-finalists United go into the weekend with a midweek glow.

Tony Pulis has managed many games in England, he tells us. None on a Thursday night though, until now. In a new excuse for failing to get any shots anywhere near the goal, WBA's manager blamed the day of the week for his team's short comings. Sanchez scored twice, Arsenal fans protested at Wenger and Pulis tried to unscramble his brain from the break in routine.

25th April 2016
Ah, the FA Cup. Back in the day, winning the FA Cup would be enough for a club. The league wouldn't matter if the club won the old trophy. Mind you, back in those days semi finals were played at grounds like Villa Park or Old Trafford and not needed to pay the rent at Wembley. Bobby Martinez still lives in this world. I am sure when he reflects on his time at Wigan he will talk of how they defied the odds to beat Manchester City at Wembley, forgetting that he also got the club relegated. Somehow, that got him a job at Everton, where this season's league performance has been far from satisfactory according to most fans. Yet Bobby is a dreamer. He believed that all would be forgiven when Everton win the FA Cup at the end of May. Yet a spanner has been thrown in Bobby's works. That spanner was Phil Jagielka. It was a miracle Everton's captain was even on the pitch following a hamstring injury, let alone lasting ninety minutes and playing pretty well considering.

Sadly for Phil there were three minutes injury time to contend with and that split second hesitation and failure to intercept Herrera's pass, no doubt down to fatigue, cost Everton a place in the final. Martial skipped away and scored the winner with the clock showing 90+2. Still, that clears the way for David Moyes to return and undo all the pretty football that we have seen at Goodison in the last two seasons, hey?

Sunday's guests had slightly less distance to travel to get to Wembley. Palace and Watford got the opportunity to size up the famous new old stadium in the second semi final. Neither team has had the greatest of 2016's to date, having got all their Premier League homework completed before Christmas, allowing them to enjoy the rest of the season whilst the likes of Norwich and Sunderland stress over last minute assignments. Palace took an early lead through Bolasie, to see their slender grasp on the game disappear soon after half time. Deeney, Mr Watford himself, equalised shortly after the break only to watch aghast as Connor Wickham scored a rare goal to book Palace into a repeat of the 1990 final.

Many a Liverpool fan has commented in recent weeks that Sahko has finally started to look like a quality footballer. Well, at least we all know how he has achieved that now! The clue might have been in the way he celebrated his Merseyside Derby goal with teammate Kolo Toure, he of a previous six month ban for "accidentally" taking a fat-burning drug that UEFA are not that keen on. Liverpool's French central defender failed a drugs test after the Europa League match against United, meaning he is facing his own six month ban from football. Maybe Kolo wasn't the guy to turn to in the changing room after all, especially as the experienced Ivory

Coast player must now stand a chance of taking young Sahko's place. Devious Kolo, devious. Liverpool have elected not to select him until his fate is decided. In the week, and following the derby victory, King Klopp described the way he is to manage Daniel Sturridge as getting the best out of an orange. Apparently, and who am I to question the German's wisdom on matters of fruit, the way to get the best out of an orange is to squeeze them gently, not to remove all the juice in one go. I think this is clever manager speak for "Daniel, get used to the bench son. You are an injury waiting to happen, so you're going to get the odd half an hour here and there." Still, King Klopp made some lovely OJ out of Sturridge this weekend, the striker scoring after 90 seconds to put Liverpool ahead against Newcastle. Liverpool led 2-0 against their former manager, Rafa Benitez – a man never believed to have likened his players to fruit, more likely soulless employees. Still, whatever methods Rafa is employing at St James Park are starting to work. Newcastle recovered from 2-0 to grab a shock point, continuing to up the pressure on the likes of Norwich and Sunderland.

Sunderland got the point they needed against Arsenal. Not the point that saves their season, but the point that moves them out of the relegation zone. I'd love to have many interesting facts about the match, but just imagine Big Sam lining up a team against Arsenal happy to take a point. Are you imagining it? Great, then you can understand why I have very little to report.

Following Villa's fate being sealed Joleon Lescott, who has done a marvelous job of endearing himself to Villa fans this season, commented that relegation "was like a weight has been lifted off the players." Judging his performance against Southampton, that weight being lifted hasn't helped Joleon run any faster or mark players any tighter as the defender was at fault for all four of Southampton's goals. Credit to Villa, they threw off the shackles and managed to score two of their own, but with Southampton also hitting the woodwork twice 4-2 was closer than it should have been.

Chelsea smashed Bournemouth 4-1. Chelsea's performance was almost as if Eden Hazard and Cesc Fabregas had come to the conclusion that if they actually want to get a transfer away from the club then they need to remind the clubs with a bit of money to spend that they do still know how to play football. Hazard scored twice and Fabregas had a hand in anything decent Chelsea strung together.

If there was a trophy for the side "most keen never to play in the Europa League" it surely has to go to Stoke City. They followed up their 4-0 defeat at Spurs, which I am pretty sure followed a 4-0 defeat to Liverpool with a 4-0 defeat to Manchester City. Lads, I am pretty sure you are safe from Thursday night football now, maybe give the fans a reminder of some of the football you played earlier in the season?

What better way to end this week than talking about Leicester City? Vardy was banned for the match against Swansea, which surely meant that Leicester were finally going to fall apart. Surely the thing we have been waiting for since, oh I don't know, November was about to occur. Ulloa could never take the England front man's place, the football pundits said. Ranieri would surely be better throwing young Gray into the mix, as his pace was similar to that of the suspended top scorer. Ranieri is not that grey for nothing you know, it belies a very wise manager. Ulloa had shown nerves of steel to equalise against West Ham last week, so had shoulders broad enough to take the weight of Vardy's absence. Swansea, managed by Ranieri's old friend Guidolin, kindly got out of the way and allowed the Foxes to put four past them. Mahrez, back to his sparkling best, opened the scoring with Albrighton finishing the job. The other two? Ulloa of course, allowing Ranieri to give us another flash of that smile of his.

Tottenham, it's over to you once more.

1st May 2016
For the first fifteen minutes at Old Trafford it looked like Leicester were determined to eke out a little more drama, as if this season has not seen enough already. United stormed out of the blocks in a way that suggested LvG had already been sacked and scored the goal that most neutrals didn't want to see. Leicester were on the rocks, their title bid crumbling before their very own eyes if you were to believe the narrative on social media. That Leicester, no backbone in the big games hey? Not true sir, not true. Before the Leicester fans were able to start taking their "we are staying up" banners seriously Wes Morgan headed home the equaliser, beating Rojo to the ball with the age old trick of standing still long enough. That Rojo, genuinely he could lose the guy he is marking in a lift. Leicester sprung into life, and even a late second yellow for Danny Drinkwater could not deter them getting the point they would have happily accepted before the match. But what are two yellow cards for the smallest of offences these days, when you are allowed to elbow and punch someone and not even give away a free kick. For me,

video referees need to be brought in tomorrow, if only to be solely trained on the frame of Felliani for the whole season. By my reckoning he would get a red card every 63 minutes if someone actually watched him. By the time you read this, it could all be over with Eden Hazard and Cesc Fabregas very keen to turn over Spurs on Monday night. They really want to see Gary Lineker in his pants and anything other than a Spurs win will grant them that somewhat dubious pleasure.

I can imagine the pre-match chat in the away dressing room at Watford. "Lads, come on. Let's give the fans something to cheer for once. Just put in a decent ninety minute shift, will you?" Well Villa very nearly did that, but decided to clock off with 89 minutes and 52 seconds on the board at Vicarage Road. Leading 2-1 against Watford but down to ten men, they contrived to lose the match 3-2 and found yet a new depth to plunge to. Troy Deeney, showing Gabby Agbonlahor what a proper captain of the team you love looks like, scored with eight seconds remaining and then again two minutes later, deep into injury time to hopefully relieve some of the pressure on his boss, Flores. Villa however, it remains to be seen what comedy they can conjure up before the season finishes.

Talking of captains being superb for the clubs they love, step forward Mark Noble of West Ham. His brace, including a fantastic volley, helped the Hammers see off WBA 3-0 and maintain their push to bring European football to the Olympic Stadium next season. What does Noble have to do to get near the England set up? There is more chance of Roy asking David Beckham, Bobby Charlton and Nobby Styles to come out of retirement before calling upon the East End legend.

Bobby Martinez often sees things in a slightly different way to the rest of the world, which is not always a bad thing, but even he must have noticed that significant amounts of Everton fans would like to see him leave in the summer. The day started at Goodison Park with a very moving tribute to the victims of the Hillsborough tragedy, following the midweek news that the jury had ruled the 96 lives claimed had been taken unlawfully. Liverpool as a city have been united in the fight for justice. The day ended with 200 or so fans remaining after the 2-1 victory over Bournemouth to make their feelings clear on their rose-tinted-spectacled manager who called the win "one of the best performances of the season." That, my dear Roberto, is like picking your favourite in Britain's Got Talent. None of them are any good, but that one will do I guess.

Mark Hughes has been linked with the soon to be vacant job on Merseyside and clearly felt it would do his interview some good if Stoke started playing a bit of football again. They led Sunderland right up into injury time, before a cool Jermain Defoe penalty rescued a point of Big Sam's men. In normal circumstances, Sunderland would have considered that a point well gained but with Newcastle beating Palace 1-0 the ante has been very much put in a lift and sent to the 8th floor. Rafa's revival continued at St James Park, the winning goal coming from a wickedly curling free kick by Spurs reject Andros Townsend. Palace missed a penalty shortly after, Darlow making a potentially season changing "save" from ex-Newcastle captain Cabaye. If that penalty had happened in Italy, a few questions would being asked, I assure you.

With all these points being gained around them in the relegation zone, Norwich must have felt they were in with a big shout in the Saturday evening game at the Emirates. Arsenal fans conducted a protest as half-arsed as their team's efforts this season, suggesting that it might be time for their legendary manager to call it a day. Arsenal signed Petr Cech to be the piece in the jigsaw that saw Arsenal finally throw off the shackles of 4th place and progress upwards. Three fine first half saves did precisely that, as he was single handedly responsible for winning the Gunners three points, which saw them move up to a lofty third. Norwich, having dominated the first half, were given an early slap in the face in the second period, Danny Welbeck sending Roy Hodgson a personal reminder of his existence with the winner. As if your place is in doubt Daniel, Roy will almost certainly value your handful of goals in a season of failure much higher than title winning and title challenging efforts from Messrs Vardy and Kane.

King Klopp is in crisis. That's two defeats in a row now for Liverpool, following their late 1-0 loss in Villarreal with a 3-1 whooping against Swansea. Does he care? Not even a little bit as Jurgen has placed all his eggs in the basket named "winning the Europa League means Champions League football next season." Even Benteke played and scored against Swansea, and if that doesn't smack of putting the reserves out I don't know what does.

Pellegrini had a tough decision to make ahead of the trip to Southampton. Play a full strength team to hopefully move back into third place and avoid a very early European start in July? Or rest the first team ahead of the second leg in Madrid on Wednesday? Having drawn the first game in Manchester

0-0, City have a puncher's chance of knocking out Real and reaching their first ever final and Pello felt this was the bigger priority probably assuming that Arsenal will find a way of losing at least one of their final two games. The gamble did not pay off, the ever impressive Southampton winning 4-2 courtesy of the standard end of season hat-trick by Sadio Mane. At the end of each season Southampton fans fill in a survey entitled "player Liverpool are most likely to buy in the summer." This year Sadio is the clear winner. Maybe Ronald can get Benteke in return?

8th May 2016
Does anyone know what odds the bookmakers were offering on Leicester to win the title this season? I haven't seen it mentioned anywhere. Equally, where on earth has this Vardy lad sprung from? The commentators really should have done a little more research on his background. Also, that good looking old Italian chap in the dugout, I am sure he has a story to tell.

At 2-0 to Spurs last Monday it looked as though Senor Bocelli might have had to cancel his flight to East Midlands Airport. The title race was heading into another weekend, the pressure was going to be on the Foxes to beat those most excellent of opposition, Everton. Yet what have we learned this season? Never ever write off Leicester's chances of doing something ridiculous. They weren't even playing in this match, they were having a shindig at Jamie's place. Yet their incredible mind control kicked in and they inspired the team in blue to play a little bit like them for the last half an hour. Hazard said he wanted to stop Spurs winning the league and boy did he prove it, curling in the equaliser that led to Ranieri "hitting the ceiling." The impossible had happened. Leicester, 2016 Premier League Champions.

With the tidal wave of plaudits coming Ranieri's way, it would have been easy to forget that there were two English teams still in European competition. By Thursday night, that had been halved. City, having defended superbly to keep Madrid to a 0-0 draw in Manchester, kind of forgot to play any form of attacking football in the second leg. In fact, the only time a City player got the ball on target it went in. Sadly for Fernando, it went in the wrong net. Madrid will have never had an easier semi-final and will face city rivals Atletico at the San Siro. King Klopp had warned Villarreal that they might be celebrating a little early, following the "Yellow Submarine's" first leg victory. 1-0 was never likely to be enough and Liverpool battered Spain's fourth best side 3-0 at Anfield to give Jurgen a second final since turning up in October.

Back to Leicester then. Shorn of Huth and Drinkwater, the newly elected Champions of England continued their week long party at the King Power by battering Everton 3-1. Jamie Vardy is a good judge of a situation, clearly believing that a hat-trick would have been greed personified on a day that was about a superb team effort. Therefore he decided to sky the penalty that would have seen him notch his third of the afternoon. Leicester's second was fittingly scored by Andy King, a youth team product that has been with the club through their administration woes. Martinez will be in charge at Everton until the fat lady sings, but the sight of a famous Italian tenor banging out his greatest hits before kickoff might be a subtle clue as to his future.

One of the greatest footballers in the world got a red card in his last ever football match. It also happened to John Terry. He has done his career his way. He will go out his way, and that way appears to be by having a party in his executive box at Stamford Bridge next Sunday. JT picked up two yellow's against Sunderland, meaning he is banned for the last game of the season which possibly means he has played his last game for Chelsea. Still, you can imagine that Terry will go "full Robert Huth" and don the full kit to wave his final goodbyes at the end of the match. Whether this does turn out to be Terry's last ever game remains to be seen, but if he does head off to the USA then we can all assume he has officially retired. Sunderland recovered from 2-1 down to beat the former champions 3-2, a win that puts the Black Cats in pole position to survive the drop. Big Sam claimed to have found meditation in the week before the game, but the victory appeared to be more down to the clinical finishing of Jermain Defoe. Zinedane Zidane was the other one, for anyone still pondering.

Sunderland's day got even better when the news from Villa Park came in. You are told something about Villa's season when the final home match extravaganza ends 0-0 but is considered one of the best results of the campaign. Newcastle, recently much improved, needed and probably expected much more than a solitary point that leaves them needing Sunderland to slip up twice.

Norwich had their chances against a United side that felt Rooney and Mata would provide the pace and work rate required to topple their relegation threatened opponents.

Louis Van Gaal had been on the genius juice again as Rooney found Mata, who slotted home the game's only goal.

It was a very emotional day at West Ham, for it was the last time the Hammers would ever play a team in white called Swansea at the Boleyn. Needing a win to keep their Champions League dreams alive, West Ham capitulated to a 4-1 defeat meaning Tuesday's match against United has everything riding on it. I, for one, will be delighted to see them leave Upton Park, mainly so everyone can stop banging on about it. I don't recall anyone being that bothered when they left their first ground back in 1893 or whenever it was.

Cup finalists Palace beat Stoke 2-1 to finally mathematically secure Premier League football next season and Bournemouth drew 1-1 with West Bromwich Albion.

Sunday saw three matches with two of them having a bearing on the Champions League places. Spurs have been notorious for being "Spursy" over the years. To lose the title to Leicester was certainly not "Spursy" but to end the season behind Arsenal after all the drama would very much be the case. Therefore Steven Davis's double in Southampton's 2-1 win at White Hart Lane opened the door for the "St Totteringham's Day" to be potentially be celebrated for the 22nd year in a row. Arsenal did not make the most of their half chance, coming from behind twice to draw with City. The single point for City stole their Champions League qualification control from their hands and sneaked it very firmly into the palms of United. As Paul Scholes says, United are in danger of being the new Arsenal. He means winning the FA Cup and coming fourth folks, keep up. Liverpool reserves saw off Watford 2-0.

A warm welcome to fans of Burnley and Middlesbrough. Both teams won promotion from the Championship at the weekend, Burnley sealing the title with a 3-0 win over Charlton. Sean Dyche is back with that ginger goatee, and will be joined by former Madrid defender Aitor Karanka, if he manages not to fall out with his entire squad between now and August. Boro broke Brighton hearts leaving the South Coast side to roll their dice in the play off lottery.

13th May 2016
The biggest disappointment in the last week of football? Nobody mentioned that a London side will soon be leaving their historic home of a hundred or so years. Yes, that's right. Tottenham Hotspur are now down to their last thirty, or thereabouts, matches at White Hart Lane before they go and rent a massively overpriced white elephant of a stadium. Does that sound familiar to anyone? Granted, at least Spurs are building their own to move into after lodging at Wembley.

Oh, and West Ham fans gave the club a typical East London send off on Tuesday night against United. Manchester United's players have come in for a lot of criticism this season, but getting grief over how they reacted to some tomatoes being thrown at their team coach as they tried to navigate through Green Street is a new one. To be fair, whilst Hammers fans "attacked" United's coach before the game, United's fans waited until after the game to attack United's coach, Louis van Gaal who watched his side concede from two late set-pieces and succumb to a 3-2 defeat. Maybe it was the sight of missiles being thrown in their direction that sent the United players back to those traumatic moments of a few hours earlier? Their failure to hold on to their 2-1 lead means that United now need an 18 goal swing in their final game against Bournemouth if they are to pip City to the final Champions League spot. A cynic would suggest United are never going to score 18 goals in the second half.

Following their 3-0 defeat to Sunderland, now-former Everton manager Bobby Martinez claimed his players were "100% behind him and fighting for him." To coin the famous managerial quote, you'd be better off having them in front of you where you can see them Bobby. They were behind you, leaving quietly through the back door as you collected your P45. As the final whistle went the Canaries died and, taking the Geordies back to their mining days, Canaries dying is normally a sign of impending doom. Sunderland's win consigned both Norwich and Newcastle to Championship football next season. Still, at least Mike Ashley bowed to supporter pressure and spent that £80m on new players. Norwich's 4-2 win against Watford was far too little too late and Rafa will be wondering how on earth his side failed to beat Aston Villa. Still, credit has to go to Big Sam and not just for his granddad dancing on the pitch after the game. He has maintained his proud record of never being relegated, shown the world that Jermain Defoe can play up front on his own and managed to send down one of the clubs that somewhat unjustly sacked him for not playing "the right brand of football." That's right Newcastle fans, one former manager stays up whilst your club goes down. Oh, and that guy Pardew you also hounded out? He's in the FA Cup Final. Well done.

The Pozzo family, owners of Watford amongst other clubs, decided that Sanchez Flores had not done enough to earn a contract extension, meaning the best looking manager in the league will be leaving at the end of the season. The news launched a social media outcry, these foreign owners not knowing how to run a club! These foreign owners have managed to keep Udinese in Serie A for two decades, taken Granada from Segunda B to six consecutive years in La Liga and have got Watford into the richest football league in the world. For me, that is enough evidence that they probably know a little bit more than the keyboard warriors. Even Watford fans who go and watch the side each week are a little relieved that a change is to be made, as the football hasn't been that great this side of the Queen's speech.

Chelsea and Liverpool drew 1-1 and Liverpool did a good job of pretending to care for most of the match considering their real interest is the Europa League Final against Sevilla. As for Chelsea, they have offered John Terry a one-year extension to his contract. Doing what, exactly, is unclear but I am sure Conte can find a job for him somewhere. Maybe club PR?

All those goings on meant that there was not a great deal to sort out in the weekend's fixtures, other than West Ham, United and Southampton all hoping to finish in the Europa League or in United's case still steal 4th base. Spurs finish their season hoping not to finish 3rd in a two horse race, so head over to part two of this week's TFTTF to see how it all ended.

15th May 2016
Manchester United's home match with Bournemouth was postponed following the discovery of a suspect package in one of the stands. No, it wasn't a first half goal but it was the most

exciting thing to happen at Old Trafford this season. Personally, I felt very sorry for all those United fans that had travelled from all over the country to support their side. The match was abandoned on police advice. If only people at United had been capable of taking advice earlier in the season Jose might have led them to the Champions League places. I think they saw City go 1-0 up and thought "stuff it, let's have the weekend off." Apparently Bournemouth went straight home, but United kicked off anyway. After 45 minutes it was still 0-0! All jokes aside, the suspect package turned out to be a mobile phone attached to some gas wires and the local bomb squad was called in to carry out a "controlled explosion." The device was thought to be a forgotten "training device." To be fair, the bomb squad showed a better ability to control anything than Wayne Rooney has all season.

Tottenham fans, a question if I may. How do you feel now the season is over? Fantastic as you finished third, which has to be at least two places higher than expected? Or hanging your heads in shame that Arsenal, for about the fiftieth season in a row, finished above you in the table? A few weeks ago Spurs followers will have been looking at the fixture list and thought "Newcastle away last game of the season, Leicester are at Chelsea. Tell you what, if we are still in the race on the last day I fancy this." Newcastle gave Rafa Benitez something extra to think about over the next couple of weeks by taking the opposition apart 5-1. Yes, 5-1! Rafa has a decision to make now, but do not forget he lives in Liverpool and a small club down the road have a vacancy.

The way Arsenal's season has gone it would have been no surprise if they had managed to completely fall apart and not take advantage of Tottenham's slip. But no, one thing Arsene's teams are still good at is putting their North London rivals back in their place and they strolled to a 4-0 win over Villa. I would imagine Arsenal fans looked at Villa on the last day when they topped the table around Christmas and thought, "Villa at home last game? If we are still in it..." Then they remembered that they would probably crumble at some point.

Chelsea were the perfect hosts to the new champions, forming a guard of honour as Leicester took to the field. Leicester thought it would be nice to give us the kind of performance that made them champions. No, not racing away and winning against the odds. Going behind, leaving it late and then fighting back with some true champion spirit. England hopeful Danny Drinkwater fired in a late equaliser following a totally disputable Fabregas penalty.

The last time Everton won anything Joe Royle was in the dugout. Following the departure of Bobby Martinez, they turned to their former FA Cup winner to provide some last game of the season happiness to the Goodison faithful. Norwich, already down, were more than happy to be the fall guys as Everton showed they can defend a bit as well as play some nice attacking football. The game ended 3-0 to the home side.

West Ham ended their season with a disappointing 2-1 loss at Stoke, meaning that Southampton's clinical 4-1 win against Palace was enough to see the Saints grab a Europe League spot at the last. The Hammers will now have to hope that

United beat Palace in the FA Cup Final to enter the EL in the qualifying rounds.

Liverpool warmed up for their trip to Basel with a 1-1 draw at WBA. The Reds had much bigger things on their mind, understandably. Sunderland probably still had alcohol on their mind but still managed to get a 2-2 draw with Watford, who presumably will be announcing their new manager sometime soon.

So that's it for the Premier League season folks, and what a season it has been. Who would have thought when we started off on this journey together thirty eight matches ago it would have ended like this? What, wait, Manchester United have to play Bournemouth still? Ok, no doubt that will get a mention when they decide to reschedule. Next week we will look back at the Europa League final, the FA Cup Final and all have a good laugh at Roy when he picks Rashford ahead of Defoe and Rooney ahead of everyone. That said, by the time you read this you will probably already be chuckling as the Euro 2016 squad is announced on Monday. Being so fine at predictions (Leicester and West Ham to go down you may recall) I am banking on Walcott out, Wilshere in and Andy Carroll politely telling Roy that he would rather head off to Dubai than be on the waiting list. The motley crew will be in action next Sunday against Turkey and I am sure you are all as thrilled as I.

22nd May 2016
Today we draw a line on all things domestic for the 2015/16 season. Which is how Louis van Gaal feels, I can tell you.

In another move of sheer class by the lurker in the shadows, Mourinho's camp provided evidence on Saturday night that the Portuguese manager had signed a pre-contract with United stating that LvG would be fired if he failed to deliver Champions League football and that Jose would take over. Failure to honour the pre-contract would cost United £3m big ones. Now regular readers will know, I've given van Gaal a bit of a kicking over the season but a man who has won what he has won over the years deserves a little more respect, even if he does think Ashley Young is an acceptable choice as a centre forward. Does Mourinho fit the mould of a United manager? They are a club who are so brand conscious they have an official partner for toilet paper so I would suggest that signing a manager who is only interested in his own image is probably not the best move. Who knows, maybe United will just give Mourinho £3m and stick with Van Gaal (and face the wrath of the United fans who seem to think Jose will give them thrilling attacking football in a team full of academy graduates).

Anyway, United won the FA Cup in extra time. Or rather, Palace lost the FA Cup with ten minutes left on the clock. Local boy Puncheon climbed off the bench in a manner that put Ian Wright back in the nation's thoughts and fired the South London side ahead with just twelve minutes to go. To be fair to Pardew, United deserved their equaliser once the replays of the Palace manager's celebratory dance were shown. Fewer moves than Wayne Rooney, that guy. Then Rooney picked the ball up deep in midfield and, in slow motion, weaved past several red and blue shirts before putting in a decent cross to the far post. Mata fired home the goal that United deserved, having hit the post twice. The winning goal belonged to another substitute, Lingard rifling home an unstoppable strike to give United their first trophy since Ferguson, signalling the start of the Mourinho circus act.

Palace were not the only side to clasp defeat out of the jaws of victory this week. Liverpool, dominant in the first half against Sevilla in the Europa League Final will have left the changing rooms after half time with the words of Klopp jangling in their ears. "Keep it tight boys, don't concede early and they will run out of ideas." Oh Jurgen, to see Moreno squeeze two mistakes into the first thirty seconds of the second period must have been heartbreaking. Still, when you have lost four cup finals in a row you must be used to cup final heartbreak. Sturridge sent a nod in the direction of Roy with a fine outside of the boot finish to give Liverpool the lead and then an entirely different team played out the second forty five minutes. Still, Kolo Toure looked half decent which was a surprise to say the least.

Speaking of Roy, he fired up the computer and typed out 27 names under the bold heading of "provisional squad for Euro 2016." They actually appeared to be 27 names not drawn out entirely at random. Rashford was given a chance to impress, Andros Townsend earned a recall ahead of Walcott due to his good form at the end of the season. Fabian Delph should be looking nervously over his shoulder at the sight of Danny Drinkwater mouthing "I've had your title and now I'm having your England shirt" at him. Unsurprisingly Wilshere was given a chance, with Henderson but it would be fool hardy to select both in the squad with their recent injuries.

Old school sticker album providers Panini got it all horribly wrong, including Phil Jones, Oxlade-Chamberlain, Baines,

Luke Shaw, Walcott and Welbeck in their print run. That's 30% of the squad wrong, yet still marginally better than my Premier League predictions for the season. Following the squad announcement, Rooney said he was happy to play "in any position for his country." If you are that committed to the cause Wayne, why not retire and let some players that can actually run have a go now? I know he beat five players in the lead up to United's FA Cup equaliser, but he was hardly moving like Usain Bolt. Clearly taking inspiration from Leicester, Sven has claimed that "England can win the Euros!" The report missed out the bit where he said "because I am clearly no judge of an England team whatsoever." Having said that, a punter stands to win £500,000 if England do indeed win, which with the odds being several trillion to one means he must have staked less than a penny.

So Roy's hopefuls took on Turkey at the Etihad on Sunday night. Vardy, given leave of absence for the next game due to attend his wedding, grabbed a late winner in a match where England looked as dangerous in defence as they did going forward. Still, if they play like this in France then they will be enjoyable to watch for once. That said, it only takes one player to slow down the exuberant attacking play, right? Vardy cancelled his wedding last year when Hodgson called him up, so the England manager had no qualms in letting him have a day off to tie the knot. The partnership with Kane, who scored the opening goal and missed a penalty, looks full of potential. England will be pleased with their 2-1 win.

Something to finish with...
At the start of the season I wrote the following preview for the season that was about to start. Fortunately, the Costa Blanca People didn't publish it. Still, what an opportunity we have now to go back over it and review the preview!

The Standard Preview of the Premier League.
You'd be disappointed if you didn't get one, it's just like an advent calendar! I plan to set it out in the style of Tony Pulis' WBA – solid, structured, minimal imagination but gets the job done. I could have embarked on a more Jose Mourinho style, offending everyone that I come into contact with, leaving a general bad taste in the mouth but still winning everything, and I also ruled out an overly idealistic Arsene Wenger approach, sticking to my plan no matter what, ignoring the facts in front of me and only having a plan A up my sleeve.

Anyway, we digress. Who is up for a bit of alphabetical order in the Premier League? Good, then we shall begin.

AFC BOURNEMOUTH
That surprised those of you that thought we would kick off with Arsenal, didn't it? Having made it clear that he plans to buy British, Eddie Howe has so far invested in an Australian, a Pole, a Frenchman, a Ghanaian, a Norwegian and a solitary Englishman. To be fair to the Bournemouth boss, all of them come with a huge wealth of English league experience. Distin maybe getting on a bit, but he might be the man to marshal the Bournemouth defence to mid-table. A lot will depend on whether front man Callum Wilson can make the step up to the top level and score goals, and Harry Arter will look to build on

a season that saw him rewarded, if you can call it that, with a few days being shouted at by Roy Keane.

My prediction: 14th
Actual finish: 16th
Difference: -2

Tell you what, if I am as close with all of them (and I already know I am not) then I will be a happy man. Bournemouth impressed in their first season in the Premier League and were never really in relegation trouble. Still, it helps if you have a manager with a plan and some money to spend. Well, it helps Bournemouth more than it helps Manchester United.

ARSENAL
Arsenal fans have been screaming many things at Arsene over the last few years, some of them just plain rude, but they must finally be delighted that the experienced manager has signed a world-class goalkeeper. A cynic might say if he had done this five seasons ago Arsenal might have won a title or two by now, but better late than never eh, Arsene? Petr Cech can only inspire confidence behind a defence that started to look quite solid last season. At the time of writing no other signings have been made and the Community Shield victory, albeit far from a guide to the season ahead, will give Wenger hope that there is a title challenge in his squad.

My prediction: 3rd
Actual finish: 2nd
Difference: +1

Hey, I am good at this! In the pure nature of a league table, Arsenal made progress this season but it sure doesn't feel like it to the majority of their fans.

ASTON VILLA

Twitter is a marvelous thing. It can give you some incredible insight in one moment, and then force the ramblings of a madman on you the next. I mean, one Tweeter said that he could see Villa being a top-ten side this season. Maybe he hadn't realised they avoided relegation last season. Sherwood has lost his main man, Benteke, to Liverpool, his second main man, Delph, to Manchester City and his "rarely seen since becoming manager but used to score lots of goals years ago man" Darren Bent to Derby. But he did get a pretty sizeable wad of cash in return, not for Bent obviously. He went on a free. With about £50m big ones burning a hole in Tiger Tim's pocket, he has set about re-investing it in such talents as forgotten City defender Micah Richards, forgotten City winger Scott Sinclair and his potential ace-card, Jordon Ayew. Ayew, signed from Lorient in France, is the man that they hope will replace Benteke's goals and not Darren Bent's. Rumours still swirl that Sherwood wants to go all crazy and sign Adebayor from Spurs.

My prediction: 15th
Actual finish: 20th
Difference: -5

Maybe they should have kept Tim. Maybe he should have signed Adebayor?

CHELSEA

What can you say about Chelsea? They've replaced Drogba with Falcao, Cech with Begovic and signed another young hopeful that will be loaned out for the season. Are they stronger than last year? Possibly. Will others overtake them this season? Probably not.

My prediction: 1st
Actual finish: 10th
Difference: -9

Oh come on, nobody saw this happening. I mean, a few saw Mourinho self-combusting, but nobody saw the champions falling this far from grace.

CRYSTAL PALACE

He is a wily fox that Alan Pardew. Picking up Cabaye for about £14m? Potential genius. Bamford deserves a chance at Premier League level so it will be interesting to see if he delivers. If he can get Connor Wickham and remind him how good he used to be, Palace could be this season's surprise package.

My prediction: 8th
Actual finish: 15th
Difference: -7

Let's just say Bamford did not deliver and Palace were not a surprise package. Actually, that is not strictly true. They did surprise several people, falling from joint fourth to nearly getting involved in the relegation battle.

EVERTON
Each season a club that you might not think would struggle tends to struggle. Welcome to this season's club. Quite frankly, if Roberto Martinez was called Bobby Martin he would not still be managing in the Premier League. Bill Kenwright fell in love with the smart looking Spaniard, but not all loves are right for you Bill. Time to get shot. Everton have signed Cleverley, predominantly because he had a half decent season at Wigan a few years ago, and Deulofeu, which actually might be a decent signing. The Toffees will hope that we see the Drogba version of Lukaku this year and not his slightly more seen version, the Emile Heskey.

My prediction: 13th
Actual finish: 11th (but they sacked Martinez)
Difference: +2

I'm actually pleased with that preview, not a million miles out at all!

LEICESTER CITY
I cannot comment on the reasons that Nigel Pearson lost his job, but they cannot be for footballing ones having saved them from the clutches of relegation last season. Some genius on the board clearly feels "The Tinkerman" is the man to take the club in a new direction though. I agree, and that direction is down. Mr Lineker, I know you won't like this, but I cannot see a Cambiasso-less side avoiding the drop this time.

My prediction: 19th
Actual Finish: 1st!
Difference: +18

Well, at least I didn't say they would finish bottom.

LIVERPOOL

Brendan has sold his "best player" and has lots of money to rebuild the squad. Does this sound familiar? He will hope Benteke is not a more expensive version of Ballotelli and that Firminio is a rare example of a Brazilian that does well in the Premier League. No Champions League qualification will mean no more Brendan.

My prediction: 5th
Actual Finish: 8th
Difference: -3

Well, there is no more Brendan.

MANCHESTER CITY

City needed a major facelift this summer. Instead they bought Delph, Sterling and Roberts. Many will think that Sterling is a step in the right direction. He might be. But the side needed at least four more fresh faces to compete for the title. Delph will not win them the Premier League and Roberts might have a major impact on their U21 squad.

My prediction: 4th
Actual Finish: 4th
Difference: 0

Well knock me down quicker than Jamie Vardy. I called one right!

MANCHESTER UNITED

Now Louis has educated Ed Woodward in the art of signing a player, United will be stronger this season. Depay, Darmian, Schweinsteiger and Schneiderlin all strengthen the starting eleven. If De Gea goes, that could be the six-point difference that sees Chelsea pip them to the title.

My prediction: 2nd
Actual Finish: 5th
Difference: -3

It is fair to say the love affair I started with Louis van Gaal back in 1995 when he was coach of Ajax is 100% over now. Never has a team bored me so much, and I am including anything by Tony Pulis in that statement.

NEWCASTLE UNITED

For once, Newcastle fans might actually be optimistic. Ashley has spent some cash on some talented young players that he will make profit on in the future. However, if McLaren can eek out some performance from the likes of Sissoko, Cisse, Perez and the three new faces Mbemba, Mitrovic and Wijnaldum then
Newcastle might start to put last season behind them. Or, it could all be another Stevie Mc car crash.

My prediction: 9th
Actual Finish: 18th
Difference: -9

In my defence, which is stronger than Newcastle's was for most of the season, I did say it could be another Stevie Mc car crash.

NORWICH CITY
Relegated, next! You want to know why? Alex Neil is a fine young manager, and the four signings he has made will all improve the squad but they are still not good enough.

My prediction: 20th
Actual Finish: 19th
Difference: +1

Even I didn't think Villa would be worse than Norwich.

SOUTHAMPTON
Oh Ronald, why don't you come here and tell me your secret? How do you do it? You sell your best players, then as if by magic – poof! More good players appear in your squad. Schneiderlin and Clyne have gone, and the money has been spent very well. Watch out for Jordi Claasie. He is very, very good.

My prediction: 6th
Actual finish: 6th
Difference: 0

Boom. Mind you, even a broken clock is right twice a day.

STOKE CITY
I went to Uni near Stoke, so I think I am qualified to say that the season ahead looks about as exciting as the city itself.

There will be some great nights out, sure, but generally it will pretty standard fare and not much to write about. Hughes has them playing differently to Pulis, but the results will be the same. Having said that, Afellay and Bojan on the same pitch could be good to watch.

My prediction: 11th
Actual finish: 9th
Difference: +2

Afellay and Bojan were very nice to watch on the same pitch at times, and this is far from my worst prediction.

SUNDERLAND
The Mackems must continue to be very grateful to Mrs Advocaat. Her husband is the only reason I am suggesting they might not get relegated. The squad still isn't very good, but the Dutchman showed last season that he could get results out of a team that has Wes Brown and John O'Shea in it. Incredible. The proposed signings of Yann M'Vila and Leroy Fer will not sell anymore season tickets, but will add some needed steel to the heart of the midfield.

My prediction: 17th
Actual finish: 17th
Difference: 0

Ok, so it didn't happen the way I expected but I was bang on with Sunderland.

SWANSEA CITY

Mr Monk, beware the second season syndrome. You did very well last season, this season you probably won't. Andre Ayew might finally fill the Wilfied Bony shaped hole in the attack. Then again, he might not.

My prediction: 12th
Actual finish: 12th
Difference: 0

I have no idea how they ended up giving me a correct prediction, but I will take it.

TOTTENHAM HOTSPUR

A worryingly quiet summer for Spurs, they have only signed three players and two of them are defenders! Yes, everyone thought White Hart Lane needed another right back, so good luck Kieran Trippier. The Poch will be looking to the Champions League places, but I believe he will be looking up at them from the dreaded Europa League positions.

My prediction: 7th
Actual finish: 3rd
Difference: +4

Fair play to the Poch, he surpassed many people's expectations for the season. I genuinely hope they push on next season.

WATFORD

Watford fans, I am sorry. I don't have enough words left to be able to tell you about the entire goings on this summer. You have a new manager and about 213 new players, some might be good, I don't know! Having scrolled down the list it appears Vydra is back, again. They say you should never go back, certainly not twice. However, the element of confusion has me thinking you might just survive.

My prediction: 17th
Actual finish: 13th
Difference: 0

Hang on, didn't I say Sunderland would finish 17th? Yes, this is how bad this preview was.

WBA
Tony Pulis has made two very Tony Pulis like signings in James Chester and James McLean. Therefore WBA will continue to play like a Tony Pulis side and will no doubt end up safe in mid December.

My prediction: 10th
Actual finish: 14th
Difference: -4

I actually have nothing to say about WBA, my second least favourite team to watch this season.

WEST HAM
If you have Sam Allardyce as your manager you rarely get relegated. If you have Slaven Bilic as your manager, you run a very high risk of being relegated. I'm sorry, I have never seen what the Bilic fuss has been about. His Croatia team stopped England going to Euro 2008, but that England side was

dreadful. It was also seven years ago. Hammers, I think you are going down. Obiang and Payet are fine players, but I think they would do better under Big Sam. Bolton sacked him, they went down. Blackburn, the same. Newcastle, yes they went down too. Watch history repeat itself once more.

My prediction: 18th
Actual finish: 7th
Difference: +11

Why not end on a high, hey? Mr Bilic I got you all wrong. Good luck in your new tax payers haven next season.

So that is, as they say, that for the 2015/16 English Premier League season. What a season it was. Far too many long winded eulogies have been written to describe how magnificent it was and I genuinely do not feel any words do it justice. Yes, even the ones I have been writing down for the last year.

Just like Jose, I will be back next season. Nobody really wants him back either.

Printed in Great Britain
by Amazon